John J. Brugaletta

SELECTED POEMS

FUTURECYCLE PRESS
www.futurecycle.org

Cover photo by John Travis Brugaletta; author photo by Claudia M. Brugaletta; cover and interior book design by Diane Kistner; Gentium Book Basic text and Cronos Pro titling

Library of Congress Control Number: 2019931185

Published by FutureCycle Press
Athens, Georgia, USA

ISBN 978-1-942371-73-1

for Howard Seller, colleague and friend

Contents

Foreword..9

From
THE TONGUE ANGLES

Day of Color..13
Fishing for Words..14
Jimbo's Enormous Ball..16
A Working Marriage..18
The Sounds of Talking...22
Archeology..23
Ancien Régime Marriage..24
Eulogy...25
Bondage Love..26

From
TILLING THE LAND

An Ordinary Curtain Rod..29
Lost Leaves from the Greek Anthology..30
In the Sticks..32
The Poor Little Poems...33
The Death of Russia..34
Biography in White..38
The Search for El Dorado...39
A Proposal...40

From
WITH MY HEAD RISING OUT OF THE WATER

A Barn Too Old...43
Artemis..44
Cassandra Takes the Podium...46
Coffee Shops...48
Fortune..49
Watching Water...50
The Self-Righteous Man in the Mirror...51
The Wolf People..52
Animal Script..54
Exposed...55
Arthur on Lancelot..56
The Nurse in the Odyssey..57
Casual Chic...58
This Is Not a Marriage...59
The Good Life..60
Aged..61

Thanksgiving...62
Being Alive and Having to Die.....................................63
The Woman Who Lived Backwards...............................64
Nasty Nick and the Banker's Kinfolk............................65
Confession to Proclivities..66

From
PSALMS OF GRATITUDE AND PRAYER

Itadaki Masu...69
The Present...70
Benefits of Pain...71
Disaffirmation...72
The Comics Page...73
To Houseguests at the Emperor's Estate.......................74
Christmas..75
Acrobats..76
First Aid..77
Tulips..78
Seer...79
Teach Us to Pray...80
Eucharist...82
Side by Side...83
The Flowering of Evil...84
Kiss...85
David and Judith..86
Everything Is Otherwise...87
Awe...88
Born Again..89
Containers...90

From
PERIPHERAL VISIONS

Waste Baskets..93
Scattergun...94
Soliloquy...95
Fish to Bipeds..96
Finis..97
The Worship of Rapidity...98
Commedia Academica...99
Emily's Corner Room...100
A Common Man...101
Ovid in Exile...102
Whale Song..103
The Hypocrite's Apologia...104

Ballade for Old Trains..105
Valentine..106
Inarticulate..107
An Ideal Wedding...108
If I'd Seen Shakespeare Sleeping................................109
Mountaineering by Candlelight...................................110
Old Loves...111
A Lovers' Spat..112
The Edge of Light...113
The Thing with Feathers...114
The Dumb Man Healed...118
If Every Day Were Holiday..120
Elephant at Our Elbow...121
Flies...122

From
THE INVISIBLE GOD

The Blind Ones...127
The Camel and the Needle's Eye.................................128
Quest of the Magi..130
Assurances...131
Hand..132
Lepers..133
Consummations...134
To Seek Is to Have Found...135
Cheater's Prayer...136
From the Whirlwind..138
No Breaking Branch..139
The Invisible God..140
Heretics...141
Prayer on Going to Bed..142
Headwaiter at Cana..143
Agape Champion..144
The Incarnate One Himself...145
Making Predators...146
Church...147
Churchgoing..148
A Gem Reset..149
Sunday Morning...150
The Wedding Feast at Cana..151
Gifts of the Spirit...152
Hearing God..154
Close Shave: A Western..155
A Civil Reply to Screwtape...156

UNCOLLECTED POEMS

Jonah..159

Age and the Age...162

The Mirror Pond...163

Secret Smoker..164

Foreword

John Brugaletta is a poet of tremendous versatility. Master of the sonnet and other traditional forms, he is equally skilled in free verse. Readers will be rewarded with startling insights. How often the poems surprise us, arriving at destinations impossible to predict. Brugaletta is even—that rarity nowadays—a devotional poet who strikes up intimate conversations with God. Here is a vital contribution to American poetry, the best of an impressive body of work achieved over three decades.

—X. J. Kennedy

From

THE TONGUE ANGLES

(Negative Capability Press, 1990)

Day of Color

One day everyone in the world wore blue.
I know it sounds improbable, but I was there.
I saw it happen.

The cheddar cheese robes of Buddhist monks turned a cerulean blue.
The fiery vestments of Catholic cardinals assumed the color of some
    araucana eggs.
Almost no one contacted anyone the day before to ask what they would
    be wearing.
And yet every schoolgirl wore a cornflower blue sweater with navy skirt.
Soldiers were surprised and frightened by the baby blue of their uniforms
until they saw their officers wearing the same.
All of the black suits of Japanese businessmen became denim blue.
Housewives at their wash looked like disheveled sapphires.

Whether the sudden change was in peoples' minds
or in the cones of their eyes
or in the clothing itself,
no one has discovered.

The next day things went back to normal
except that everyone started every sentence
with the word "you."

Fishing for Words

The fisherman fishes all day for words,
words he knows are there,
words he's seen lipping the surface,
spangled and repetitive maybe,
or words just below the light,
darkened things watching.

Others had been there as the words surfaced
but didn't see them
or couldn't believe they were words
or had no way to catch them.

He rises early and under the young sky
begins angling for them, casting here, there,
in obvious places
and in the shallows where no word could swim.

He hooks one at 6,
plays it till it rises to his eyes,
nets it.
Ten minutes later he hooks a second
but just as he glimpses its first syllable
it throws the hook and sinks away.

At mid-day, where the trees darken the water,
another word bites. He has it.
It is beginning to be a phrase.
Around 7 he has the third.

The fisherman takes them home for supper
and there, as he eats them,
alone at his table,
the phrase becomes a part of him.
He says it once to himself
but it makes no sound.

Then he says it to a photograph
but it only sounds like wind.
Then he says it to the cat
but the cat has already eaten.

Finally he holds a clear canning jar to his lips
and says it.
When the words are in,
they lie on the jar's bottom,
small and dry, but their eyes still open.
They watch him as he seals the jar,
puts it on a shelf in his cellar
and leaves them to time.

Jimbo's Enormous Ball

Jimbo had a passion for foil,
the kind that lines a pack of cigarettes.
When he saw a friend take the last smoke out and crumple
       the empty pack
Jimbo would say, "You gonna throw that away?"
They all knew he wasn't asking a question.

He kept a sharp eye out for gum wrappers,
hoods off wine bottles,
the packaging from certain posh candies,
and he added them to his foil ball.
He wanted the biggest foil ball in the world.

When he married, his wife was puzzled for weeks.
Then she discovered where her aluminum foil was going.
She switched to waxed paper, but now and then foil was what she
       needed,
so she would "borrow back" some from his enormous ball.
He called it stealing, and he never forgot it.

But as Jimbo's ball grew from a baseball to a basketball to a beach ball
things got worse for him.

It may have had something to do with his mother.
About the time Jimbo was conceived
she told a neighbor she'd had a dream
that people in shining airplanes
had sprayed her with silver paint
until she was dead and had become a metallic statue.

Or it may have come from his father
who had gray eyes
and whose false teeth were all steel.

Whatever the cause, as the ball of foil grew
it soon became too large for the doorway of his house
and so couldn't leave the house without causing some damage.

A few years later it reached the ceiling, then the walls of its room.
It seemed a natural thing to him that the ceiling and walls should be
      torn down.
In the end the roof had to go.

By this time his wife had gone to live in another state
where plastic wrap is the only legal covering for food.

I drove by Jimbo's ball yesterday.
It's beginning to look like a planet.
You could hardly see Jimbo, the glare was so great.
Besides, he looked so small.

A Working Marriage

Monday

The sun shines on nothing natural more
nectarine-like in the morning than your buns
as you step out from showering. Repeated suns.
Once I thought such commonplace would bore

the liveliest esthete, but always I perk up
the way daisies do and follow with my face.
They're lower suns themselves: I see their place
so well through mist of gown that it's a tossup

whether I would have you always nude
or sometimes veiled. Gauche, you say, when lewd
eyes are around. Yes, but how when there are none?

Imagine us unfallen, you the *bonne
ménagère,* I the director. Our homespun
sporting's fine, for no innocence is rude.

Tuesday

Who's innocent, you ask? Why not I?
Is it so hard to think (when I creep up
behind you doing dishes) that to cup
one breast in either hand is not a try

at some deep-seated matter? This is play
to lighten the load of work. When you trip
over me, not knowing I was there, and my grip
makes move to save us, let's just say

my pure intentions are a gloss on the shined
floor where we lie fallen, fallen back
to basics, contact with our source, things we're blind

to when we see only orange peels and pens
chewed with worry. Who sees dust balls, black
heel marks while they're reveling in glens?

Wednesday

You're right. There's work to do. Here stands
the tiller, there the field. You think of our
autumnal needs. That trick of thought turns sour
my rollicking. I'm assiduity. My hands

first redden, then harden. Your guidance, once
half my mind, I'm blind to as this grub
in the furrow, I, stroking like Beelzebub,
all force, tight teeth, thrown weight and grunts.

Then time for lunch: the water cools my head
and hands. We sit in quilted shade and roll
on our tongues soft cheese, strawberries and bread.

Our garden glistens as we watch on his patrol
through branches a hummingbird. Once you said
what he does and I think together: "Buttonhole."

Thursday

Fantastic and cruel, the flowers you make with just
that buttonhole stitch and the silk floss laid
and couched, silver-smooth and strong as hair grayed
(like yours, or mine). So it's a sudden gust

of grave that peels our eyes to death—so what?
We'll use the shock. Put some dandelions in among
the rosebuds, grasshoppers with peacocks, all flung
together as our Maker marries torso with gut,

love spot with forgotten meals. Here am I,
your model insect. Women in summer cock an eye
at my hairy legs. You want one kicked how high?

And when you do the flowers with the weeds,
you choose the blooms; let me prefer the seeds
for neat rotundity, significance and deeds.

Friday

What do you mean is what I'd like to know.
I see you as the dream I've often had,
significant somehow. You are one dryad,
I another, roots entangled. We grow

beside a house and past a bedroom window
where they dream of us. Our limbs abrade
in the wind, then fuse. We find that we can wade
through earth now, nourished as we are below.

And so—are you the feeder or the fed?
We've lain a thousand times with crossing limbs

but when did we mix roots? In the interims
of this dream life, we floated on the bed

ourselves...ah that's the meaning: mixing roots.
Above the trees our low seeds make high fruits.

Saturday

One Saturday, the sun late, you gone,
my legs of thinking stalk our rooms. They know
our voices, moods and smells, and in the dawn
knows us upstairs in bed, the civil, slow

awakening with paper, coffee, juice, croissants.
I put together half, enough for me,
and carry through our rite. It's as if some law
within, once shunted with activity, set free

by stillness, now sets me free to play what once
I strained at as a compromise. I disliked eating here.
While you're away my soul goes exiled, hunts
everywhere your spoor, delicious deer.

It takes a while. At ten o'clock I find,
calling and hungry, your face, your gestures, your mind.

Sunday

Some say the angels pass through one another in their joy
and look down on our most penetrating thrills
as we watch dogs. They say we will enjoy
that ecstasy ourselves when all the bills

are paid, the dishes washed and our boy
has taken over things; that it will be, compared
with our coarse deeds, complete, our essence shared
and then retrieved and fused again. If quills

were coarser than word processors, I'd have dared
long ago to dump this body on the nearest trash.
But every morning when I've heard the splash
and you reach down to dry your foot, I love

this world again and flesh, even in collision.
I'll wait for what awaits me up above
till I hear greetings to abstract fields of elision.
Down here the delighted bee creeps fondly in the foxglove.

The Sounds of Talking

Soft as the sounds of cooking, as fox kits
tumbling in their den, or zebra finches called
to committee in a nearby acacia; as the ruts'
patois of rain in sodden beds, the spilled
stream, an infant babbling as it wakes,
hand shears clipping in August, footsteps
in a hall; or the passing of a flock of bikes,
a breeze, a quiet car; the cobbler's taps.

Gentle as the unhurried clatter of someone baking,
the educated knock of knives on wood,
the syllabic patter of pots, a skillet making
small talk with the kettle, what the sauce implied.
As soft as humans in their daily lives,
as gentle speech as bees, or snakes, or doves.

Archeology

Earth, make room for this, your child.
All that's left belongs to you.
No one asks that you be mild
since it was your hand that drew

all her failings to a head.
Do your worst. When she awakes
she will live and you'll be dead.
He who made this life and makes

every moment some new soul,
waits till all your venom's spent,
till disease has bored a hole
through the bones and brain, and rent

all that's agile, pretty, right.
Then he whistles, and his part—
grief and thought and breath and sight—
wakens and the two depart.

Just remember as men dig,
when this plain's a deep ravine,
in the era of the pig,
for a moment, be serene.

Tell them that she cleaned her house,
did the wash and said her prayers,
married (bad advice) a louse—
this in broken bones and hairs.

Tell them what they have are scraps
of a life as good as theirs.
Give them reason to respect
crumbling bones and fragile hairs.

Ancien Régime Marriage

Like one of those delicious summer days
when you may read until your eyelids fall
and you will drowse and doze and, all in haze,
the countryside within gives fish that graze

aslant the humid hills, and seraphs call
like trees' susurruses and horses' neighs
that wake you to soft laughter in the hall,
and you delight in book and dream and all;

so is this marriage half a daylight dream
in which we float to kiss and are ablaze
with ease, adrift in grace's glowing steam,

and half a novel of *ancien régime*
address and form, each turn of plot windfall
and we luxuriate on tea and cream.

Eulogy

She was homely as this poem, my grandmother.
She made dumplings all her life out of sympathy.
On her Kansas farm, a hen's cackle made her laugh.
(Her fallacies were all pathetic.)
When she married, she was a fresh brown egg;
when she died she was a dumpling.

Illiterate, she had by heart
the formulas for nourishment,
wove them out in gustatory poems:
flour and butter one way,
hogs' heads and mushrooms the other.
She smelled of bay leaves when she didn't smell of soap.

Her province was her house, her family,
the reputed world merely places to lose them.
Her children, by attending or ignoring her,
told her in their several codes they loved
the life she'd given and the goodness meant.
The only pay she would accept was infants,
her final reward, to be one eternally.

Bondage Love

Houdini's audiences loved him.

They were poor people, illiterates:
hod carriers, icemen, washerwomen,
undernourished kids.

They understood what it meant
to have your hands manacled,
your feet tied,
to be put in a straitjacket
then in a box
and sunk.
They knew what it was like to have no way out.

It was the way the world made love to them.

So he showed them, without a word,
that one could have no way out,
not a single, possible way out,

and get out.

From
TILLING THE LAND

(Mellen Poetry Press, 1992)

An Ordinary Curtain Rod

He was not Caius, not an abstract man,
but a creature quite, quite separate from
all others.
                              —Tolstoy

I am an ordinary man.
I think myself exceptional.
This is an ordinary trait.

When I look at my house
I think, "What a fine home.
I am better for living here."

Guests will give a compliment
now and then. When they do not,
envy suppresses their words.

I have risen social miles.
I have read and know the classics.
People tell one another my name.

Why, then, am I afraid of ladders?
I soar with intellectual giants,
yet I tremble to climb for a curtain.

Lost Leaves from the Greek Anthology

1.

Mellipus has ordered his slaves to
stop reading poetry to his guests at supper.
They listen now to chatter from Mellipus.

An economical host.
What with indigestion
they eat less.

2.

Dion, to live long,
shunned wine,
drank only water.

Here he lies
having drunk his fill
then washed up on the beach.

3.

Antiphanes caught and skewered
only five skittish lambs
while his sword saw active duty.

Now that he's hung it over the mantel
they nuzzle his hand in the street.

4.

Memnon, it seems, has heard
a legend of buried treasure.

Some oracle has told him
it lies between a woman's legs
but didn't say which woman.

5.

Cleomenes the misanthrope
bought a new robe today
thinking it will make others admire him.

It catches spittle as well as the last one.

6.

It's no use being humble
and self-deprecating
with Euphorbus.

He agrees with you.

7.

On the Areopagus
men can believe anything.

Very few do.

8.

Some who glimpse these
will think that I, Ancrises,
lived them all. Not true.

At supper, instead
of thanking the host,
they want an account of how
the onion plants were fertilized.

In the Sticks

This cabin we have rented by the lake
comes with one gray canoe and one green snake.
I greet the last at noon, the first at dawn;
one slides along the waves and one the lawn.
Now, from this wooden chair, this peeling porch,
his little lifted head is like a torch
to dimly light my final, fatal crossing.

The wind is up; my gray canoe is tossing.
From somewhere out of sight a water bird
emits a panting call that can be heard
across the lake, I'm sure, where neighbors stay
and light their lights for answer. Then a bray,
a female human cry like pain or rut
corrects my vision from the soul to gut.
They're just along the shore, that newer place,
the angry fellow and the pretty face—
Tonight, it may be, someone new is formed
and some new corner of the cosmos warmed.

Come, Master Vergil, come and read me now
your tender eclogue prophesying how
he shall be born. But change the tune, for this
you know, is not the first but monstrous bliss.

The Poor Little Poems

There are parents who haul out their daughters
when the guests have eaten and are sitting
with coffee, drag them out in their pinafores
and make them, whether they can or not, sing.

And parents whose pensive sons love to read,
alone in a quiet room, a book about travel or snakes
but are forced on their feet with a taste of blood
in their mouths, to whistle or speak or do tricks.

And the guests always sit thinking hard
of what they will say, what tone they will use
when the child is done and it's time to applaud
and how to mask their pity till leaving the place.

And then there are poets at readings
parading their poems, those shy, unhappy songs.

The Death of Russia

In a dark Leningrad basement, Abraham
Kameraz was joined by fellow scientists.

They say love is not like a potato:
you can't throw it out the window.
But I say you love what you need,
and you keep it as long as you feed
on it.
      The bombs fell, tore
through everything good, right to the core
of life: temples, bedrooms,
gardens. When something strong dooms
things like that, you want to act as fast
as you can to make things last
a little longer. The potatoes were a new
strain brought all the way from Peru
to pull our yield up by the bootstraps
from wilt. Marbles as they were, I dug
them up to the air, sacked them, tried to lug
them in the house but finally left
a third. Too heavy for me to heft
all the way to Leningrad.
Even when lightened, I still had
a job of it, believe me, over this wall
and hugging that field's edge for cover. Call
me a fool if you like, more than
once I thought myself a hero, then a man,
then at last a dunce, and then,
not having given up, a hero once again.

I got to Leningrad, my feet
in blood, no one to greet
me, no assistants, comrades,
nothing. Only rubble and some lads
who begged at first, then turned on me like
rats to take my sack. I had to strike
the starving children so my country would
not starve—supposing always that she could
survive the never-ending rain

of bombs. I gave them just enough pain
to outweigh their hunger pangs and off
they went.

       Then I heard a cough
and saw a hazy face through
a basement window. I wish I knew
what made me think, "That's it. That's the place."
I found the steps, the door, the pit, the face.
She too was seeking refuge: when she saw
me enter, all her looks went raw
that yet another man had found her.
Yet she was starving, so, like a cur,
she begged for food and snapped
at me.

       Before I left, I'd wrapped
some meat in paper, shoved in my
coat. The food I'd eaten, the paper I
still had. I thought she'd at least
get something from the fat, though hardly a feast.
She ate the paper. I watched her eating
as a father watches in those fleeting
moments when his child is transfigured
before his eyes and glows. It triggered
something in me and I caught a view
of Russia squatting in mud and forced to chew
on trash and leavings. It made my sack
more precious than ever. Then I was back
among the Incas in the Paucartambo Valley:
those mountain tubers now were in this alley
basement, and they lit it up like flame.

But suddenly my real condition came
falling in like rubble; they would rot
down here, or freeze in winter. There was a cot,
a trestle and some stools she'd found.
I broke one up and made a fire. The sound
disturbed her I could see, but then she stared
into the little flame, and we shared
a little warmth, a little solitude.

Soon the boys came back and chewed
a hole in the sack, this time real rats.
We beat them away, she and I, between chats
about whose turn it was to go for wood,
what month it was, where was a good
place to find a scrap of bread.

Then one morning she was dead.
Cold already, so it happened while I slept
my deepest, while there crept
through my brain fried potatoes fine as straw,
meat roulades, soups, fish. I saw
pashtet, botvinia, kurnik...but there, enough
of holding up what passed for bliss in my rough
circumstance for the world to mock.
I buried her in the filthy smock
she wore. As she slid into the grave,
her hand in rigor mortis sent a rigid wave,
white and fluid as a masterpiece in stone.
A month later, as I sat alone,
Kurpiensky came, then Ormulov
and others. We shooed the rats off,
built the little fires, went out
in search of food. Or rather, lout
that I was, I let them go.
Nothing seemed worthwhile. Russia was dead.
I made myself a makeshift bed
and lay, watching the window flicker day
and night, night and day, as if to say,
"One thing is like another; nothing matters now."

The war ended. They came and found us.
When they understood, it was an endless fuss
over what I'd done. There were awards.
But no one understood the cords
were cut between my life and me.

I walk the roads hoping someday I will see
my homeland. Everywhere somebody has a field
of potatoes from my sack. At home they're peeled,
boiled and stuffed down someone's maw.

Now and then some farmwife waves a paw
across a wall. Then I find a field's edge
somewhere, crawl into the cover of a hedge,
rock myself on the ground and moan
for Russia, alone.

Biography in White

Because the hospital sheets were white,
because the pillowcases and the walls were white
and the baby powder they rubbed on the newborn
        baby's skin;
because the vanilla milkshake of her adolescence
        was white as well,
and her bridal veil and wedding cake;
because all this was white
it was not easy for her to know the meaning of white.

Their stucco house was white, and the bread they ate;
the linens on which they made love,
the shells of the eggs she cracked for breakfast.
There were bandages she put on her children's knees,
a plaster cast her husband wore
after the snowy ski slopes,
the white slopes to which he did not invite her.
All were white, as were both refrigerator and range
at which she worshiped,
pale priestess that she was in her white slip.

In the end her hair
lay in white tangles on the pillow.
Flecks of foam dried at the corners of her mouth,
the mouth he once delighted in kissing.
And then, among the blue hyacinths
and red gladioluses, a small pot of narcissus,
meaning something perhaps
but nothing anyone could put in words.

The Search for El Dorado

At first it was the shores, their jungles come
down to the sea like monsters come to drink,
that put them off. But up behind, a wink
of snowy peak promised Elysium.

Somewhere a man's delight in gold was numb
with surfeit—so they'd heard—for, dusted pink
with it, he'd step into the lake, let sink
a fortune in metallic martyrdom.

They climbed the mountains steep as castle walls
but never found the fancied gilded man,
only simple villages, quetzals
with greengold tails, golden-kernelled maize,
sweet-scented valleys with waterfalls that ran
down into lakes all golden in the evening haze.

A Proposal

The farmer stumbles through the weary day
while cattle die and wheat begins to mold.
There are no guarantees that work will pay.

No matter what we wish, what we've been told,
the firmest lives and loves may not survive.
The universe ensures us nothing but the cold.

But why should we allow death to deprive
us of such minimal delight as could
come to us if we two kept alive

for...well, how long? A week? All right. Now should
we not get slaughtered by a biker gang,
eviscerated by a sleazy hood,

or bombed by enemies because we sang
"America the Beautiful," let's kiss,
let's love, and let's move in. Or, in the slang

of eighty years ago when notes like this
were commoner than now: "Be my belamour."
Who knows? We might eat several crumbs of bliss.

But keep in mind that nothing good is sure.
I say this just to keep my conscience pure.

From

WITH MY HEAD RISING OUT OF THE WATER

(Negative Capability Press, 2014)

A Barn Too Old

A barn is dying of neglect and time
a mile or so away,
more openings to wind and rain and sleet
than boards against the day.

The farmer's moved his rattling, rusted truck
from crushing's huge collapse;
the feral cats have found a safer place
to take their feline naps.

I go by once each day and watch the slow
combustion of the will
his father had when he nailed board to plank,
and many young have still.

But I can only feel what has to be
when living's light goes dim,
to have no urge to mend or plant or sing—
a half-dead, unpruned limb.

Artemis

On Crete, before the savage Greeks arrived,
I was the Lady of Wild Things. In Phrygia
I was Cybele. Ephesus was later, but I still
was mother goddess, as my many paps attested.
Only the Greeks, randy for boys and girls,
could give me paltry sacrifices as a virgin.

So when Agamemnon boasted that
his hunting skills could easily equal my own,
it was a tidy step to plot the death
of his most prized and virgin daughter.
He needed winds to carry his fat fleet to Ilium,
winds that would avenge the ravaged honor
of his bested brother, winds that I reversed,
sequestered and confused. Let him hunt
for ways to put a thousand ships
on Troy's windblown and flatland beach,
hunter that he boasts of when there's peace.

The oracle sat her tripod, went entranced,
and I sent mumblings of my target trade:
a simple sacrifice to bring fair winds Troyward,
and for no more than one daughter, Iphigenia.
Then Calchas interpreted these mutterings.

The king, this son of lies, would have a choice
stewed in futility, ignominy at his impotence
to move the ships, or in the end be drained
of lifeblood by maddened Clytemnestra,
made murderous by mother-love.

And so the richest Greek, this mulish Mycenaean,
snared in his royal robe, would be chopped down
like a tree by his wife's ax, and she herself
then murdered by her son, pleading with
her udders hanging out for mercy of her
bladed boy. And this it took, all this to calm

my anger at the Greeks, especially the family
of Atreus, for bullying my worshipers into
belief that I, so fertile once, am childless virgin
scouring the parched hills for pigs and deer
like some ragged beggar with a clumsy spear.

Cassandra Takes the Podium

What good is fending off a lustful god
if all it brings is rape and slavery?
No hint of those stephanic blooms that grace
the heads of skillful whores. I will admit
I led him on to think that for the gift
of prophesy I'd lend him all I'd kept
in tight-wrapped robes. My yearnings were to be
a Sibyl, to reveal the absolute
while keeping me inviolate of men.
But when I'd been filled up with seer's skills
Apollo visited, stood by my bed.
I knew he'd come to have his pay: myself.
But I said, "Sibyls babble senseless truths,
a sign that they must never bear a child,
who would in time speak living sense and clear."

This scheme unmanned his full rigidity
and he, deflated, crept his chidden way.
It was not till I knew that Paris was
to be the torch that razed the ashlar walls
of Ilium that I could see the price
Apollo seized: once gargled out, the truth
translated, Alexandrus still unstained,
I'd be no more believed than those insane.
In fact they called me so. And then when I
perceived the wooden horse was pregnant with
a troop of Greeks, a handful seconded,
the mass of Trojans saying, "Take the gift."
It was the second time my second sight
had seen invisibly the fall of Troy,
and neither was believed. As for my prim
virginity, small Ajax conquered it
by forcing me from sanctuary's bay.
And that sweet desecration of Athena's
sanctity will bring ordeals on Greeks.
May that avenge the loss of Ilium.

But I would keep my purest days today
if rank Apollo sought my bed again.
For nothing good can last, not civic pride,
or cities saved by swapping sex for gifts,
or sacred longing for a truthful life.

Coffee Shops

We stop at them on the roadside,
walk in and are relieved
that the chairs are plastic, the tables Formica,
everything orange and brown and scratched,
secure in their anachronism and imperfections,
like monks, or politeness.

The meringue on the pies
and the waitress's hair
both achieve height and elegance
by means of daily necessity.

The atmosphere is not ambience.
It is the honest flatulence of grease,
with high notes of potatoes and bacon.

The newspaper has been read
by someone who left
ten minutes ago for work.
It lies now despoiled,
as open to us
as a woman who has decided
anyone may know her without paying.

And the imitation flowers
do their best to mime
their evanescent betters.

We always have stopped at shrines like these
for a rest, or because we're hungry.

Fortune

It was a comfort not to be the Czar.
Each summer he believed would be his last,
but people took him as a lowly tar.

Still, he believed each June would be his last,
that he was sinking like his native star,
for he had had his birthright's fortune cast.

Once cast, one's horoscopic future can't be far,
and it was comforting to not be Czar,
although some things were well about the past.

His headache was that rank iconoclast
who made him think each summer was his last.
He tensed to hear the tires of a car.

And then one day, at her due time, the char
said, "Run away. They come." He was aghast.
He took his pistol, doused his cheap cigar,

then ran. The cleaning woman heard a blast.
At that same time he dreamed of caviar
and richly furnished rooms, sweet smelling, vast.

Watching Water

Follow with your eye the snowflake down,
a lightweight parachute the weight of light
until it masses, gathers minuscules
in billions and turns tall, a glacier.

And then it edges downhill like a train
that's just about, but grudgingly, to leave
a station where it stood and thought for years
with cars enough to belt the planet's waist.

And on, at regal pace, until the far
equator sends its emissaries of
the piercing sun, the love that kills, the warmth
unlocking all its cold solidity.

It calves and calves until it calves itself,
then goes to vapor where our eyesight ends.
All this we watch and say, "How beautiful!"
as if observing gladiators die.

The Self-Righteous Man in the Mirror

My mirrored face is not the face that's mine.
I'd never let pedestrians observe
my lower life, the dribble when I dine.

No doldrums! Let them see my verve.
They always keep what's worst and lose the best.
So may they keep the nothing, lose their nerve.

I scorn the tester, but I loathe the test,
for therein lies trespassing and offense.
I have full charity for all the rest:

for bossy matrons, for untidy gents,
for those who do not smile and nod hello,
for all these fools my charity's immense.

If only they would somehow deign bestow
such pure esteem on me, the world would glow.

The Wolf People

The sun had dried the ground.
You could not step without a puff of dust.
Jays screeched at the heat.
We with garbage for the midden
where the gray wolves swarmed,
picking through our leavings,
keeping an eye alert for us.

What if they did not skulk away?
What if they got used to us?
Would they stay and leap for the orts in our hands?
Whose midden would it be then?
I had seen them across the canyon eating an elk calf,
tearing off pieces before it died.
Would that be one of the People?

They turned again, slowly. Had it begun?
I dumped my basket on the pile
and that is when I saw the eyes
two tents away, staring at us. A young one.

My brother had the snake in him,
one cousin the otter, another the beaver.
It was time for me. Was wolf my totem?

Day and days I took the garbage,
at first asking, then grabbing it before the others.
I had to fight Kamput to do it.
All the People were watching me
walk among the wolves.

One day I put down a bone, a little meat still on.
A gray wolf came slow, slow, grabbed it and ran.
I knew then. Klusit was my real name, Gray Wolf.

Now the hair leaves my head,
grows from my stretching ears, grows gray.
Now the People have wolves
among the tents, because of me.

I have taken into me the wolves' ways—
fighting, feeding, playing, breeding.
Now the People come to me when they need a pup.
Now when the Other Kind attack
the wolves help us and the Other People run.

I walk among the tents.
Whatever I look at, soon it is near my tent flap—
hatchets, knives, ropes, wives.
I wake, I walk out past my gift, climb to the peak,
hold up my empty hands to show I am unarmed
and I chant thanks to the Great Wolf above.

It will be warm today. It will be good.

Animal Script

It is not true that only we can write.
The fox who steps so gingerly inscribes
his name in vulpine letters; and the elk
writes Elk across the paper we call snow.

Even the horse, subservience aside,
wears on his feet four broken signet rings
to signify, when all four feet are glue,
that he was royal once, and led his kin
to flourish on the Mongol steppes, but then
was vanquished by a weaker sort of beast,
a primate, a savannah breed too sly
for trials of brute strength, persistent too,
who nailed these iron styli to his hooves,
assigning him to write his servanthood
upon that primal page, the dust of Earth.

Exposed

Away from city lights, from fog or smog,
those cosmic glints seem brighter and more real.
It's then we see how scant a shield we have
from endless falling, and how little chance
we'd have of ever landing anywhere.

Now think of those poor hypocrites who said
that Galileo had it wrong: "If earth
rotated (God forbid!), we'd be thrown off
this naked sphere. And yet we stand, unmoved."

They saw one-half the case alone—the fright—
while Galileo wanted only facts.
And what would you or I reply if we
were faced with choosing peace or frightful truth?

Arthur on Lancelot

Of course I knew. What choice was there for me?
It was to lose him from my table, my ablest knight,
or lose a modicum of honor in the whisperings,
a trifle by comparison. Besides, he was my friend,
which counterbalanced my resentment
when I pictured them at tossing on her bed,
her joyous cries more heartfelt than
she sighed for my more nobly driven thrusts.

And I had winked at other couplings
in strange beds, one knight substituting for another,
to keep a semblance of the peace.
A king must leave aside these boyish frisks
to give his thought of statecraft better weight.
I had the table fashioned round to say
that every man was knight, and each had say,
the king reserved to give the final say.
How could I move more fiercely at my own
concern than at another's?
And yet, from that day that I knew, her face was
maculate, her voice a rasp, her hands a milkmaid's.
I took no longer sprightly to her bed.
Therein lay the poison that assassinated all.

The Nurse in the Odyssey

Yes, nursed him I did when he was but a lad,
but when his teeth got sprouted, put my dugs away.
"No more," I said, and land, did he blubber.
(My husband said, "Good chance," and had a sup.)
Went off to his uncle's for to learn manhood,
got a boar's tusk in his leg what took many
a gathering of simples to close it on the blood.

Then was that doxy Helen gone with Paris,
Left her daughter and husband away behind
for the high life in Priam's land, they say.
So all the fit Achaeans supposed to go
and get her back, with all her "charms,"
to decency. Bah, say I, let her highness choke
on cates. She's worth not one Greek boy
speared through and left to die on foreign sand.

But go he did, for trickery won't always work,
even if your name is known for it—Odysseus.
And stayed away ten year, and then another ten
when all the others sat in settles by the fire.
And she, poor soul, aweaving and ataking out
to keep the heated suitors all at bay.

Comes one, a beggar don't you know, in rags
and begs to talk to her in private-like.
Tells her Odysseus is living and is near.
She's on her guard for just such lies, but
tells me bathe the fellow, as custom is.
I do, and there's the scar the boar's tusk left.
The rest is royalty. I have no more to say.

Casual Chic

Uncle Frank would take a bath each day,
then shave and rinse his facial hairs away.
In natty suit, white shirt and a silk tie,
he'd walk out like a man who'll never die,
but live forever in a posh hotel.
The girls adored his manly, wholesome smell.

But then a Nazi with a curt mustache
began to turn his scapegoats into ash,
so Uncle Frank put off his natty suit
and donned some clothes more proper to dispute.
In olive drab, and in a Sherman tank,
he charged the Bulge, and there went Uncle Frank.

I think of him, a redhead on his arm,
a dandy who could never come to harm,
evaporated in a flash of Tiger fire,
the joy of style undone upon the pyre
of war's disorder, anger's dishabille,
the turning of the ages' wobbling wheel.

This Is Not a Marriage

Now in early morning's tentative light
it all begins to come clear—
the spoons in their drawer slots,
the flashlight where it might be needed,
my wife still asleep in our bed.

We moved here from seven climates away
not knowing if our transplanted needs
could accept the acid soil and the timid sun.
But in a week the house began to live,
its faucets standing like Renaissance servants
ready to pour out the water of many uses,
the electric outlets eager to inspire tools,
the heating here for the easy asking.

Taken alone, all this is not a marriage,
but begun in such a place,
like a plant in the loam of our lust,
it aspires to more, and it finds more as it rises
into the air, the light, the admiration.

We water it with our losses, prune it
lightly with our respect for its future,
and cater to its needs with our own need
for mercy projected onto it as a friend.

The Good Life

He told me he was grateful he'd been born
to parents who could barely pay the rent.
The smells of sewage as you climbed the stairs
or burning garbage on a summer day,
the shattered glass in hamburger that killed
the barking dog in two days' agony,
the ice man with his tongs and pee-soaked pants,
the hardly spoken prayer for privacy,
all wakened in his youth an appetite
for what was only at the city's edge—
the wide-spaced houses and the simple air.

In time, the extra bedroom lined with books,
and roses all along the garden paths,
he'd leave to lecture on what pleased him best,
returning to write sonnets on the scent
of roses on the springtime's warming air.

Aged

Forty years it had been since we
left the Green Berets. Now he puffed
toward me across the lawn, the
toned and hardened warrior of his body in
retreat from a youthful self-confidence to—
as it turned out—sagging sincerity.

We found chairs and a cocktail table,
he smoking Camels, I a Peterson pipe,
and drank Black Label on the rocks.
It hasn't left me yet how rotund
he'd become. I of course was too,
but that's because of cortisone.

He paces himself now,
accepting his softening abilities
as he must, a thing we never thought of
when we climbed, jumped, swam,
chopped, chased, marched all night,
then showered, dressed and went on dates.

Now we sat and drank and smoked.
Even our sentences were hard to finish—
correction, *his* sentences.

Thanksgiving

The sound of pie crust being pounded
and the smell of turkey dressing in the oven;
a Mozart divertimento, together with
the early seed-and-bulb catalogs.

A labrador on the kitchen floor
being licked by the tomcat who soon
tires of it, bites the dog's cheeks,
getting no response to pain, and walks away.

The day's a medley of sun and clouds,
planks of sunlight touching on the denuded
clearing to be impregnated next spring
with daffodils, foxgloves, daisies, ranunculi.

At present it is all promises, only promises.
But how much better than no promise at all.
We take them into us like food, flourishing
on their insistence that life is unquenchable.

Being Alive and Having to Die

After surviving my first eviction
into fluorescent light and
the gonging of steel pans,
this oddity of space and motions
had hardly become custom
when I learned I would one day dissolve.

One said it would be final, terminal,
all there is to it.
Another said it was one more passage
like the Bering Straits—
a narrow gate into a wider world.
A third said nothing, just went on
chopping firewood, carrying water,
as the birds went on chittering.

The Woman Who Lived Backwards

There was an old woman who lived in reverse:
She died in a crib and was born in a hearse.

In driving her car (in reverse gear of course),
She always made sure it was pushed by a horse.

Her garden grew tall with potatoes and peas,
So tall that their top leaves grew down to her knees.

She fizzled and sputtered when things were correct,
But whistled and hummed when her new car was wrecked.

The food she devoured (like ice cream and pork)
Refined her until she had legs like a stork.

She'd often set fistfuls of money on fire.
Guess what! The next day her bank balance was higher.

She read eighty books in the space of one summer,
And—wouldn't you know—in the fall she was dumber.

Her house was so spotless by noon every Friday
She brought in more trash just to make it more tidy.

She traveled each evening to where she'd been hired
And worked very hard so as not to be tired.

And then the next morning she'd hurry home fresher
To write a critique of her foe, M. C. Escher.

She turned on the light before going to bed,
Then slept with bare feet and a blanketed head.

She didn't get married but split in two pieces,
Then one of her went off to live with her nieces.

The other grew older till she was a baby.
And all of this story is partly true, maybe.

Nasty Nick and the Banker's Kinfolk

Old Nasty Nick,
He never worked a lick,
Just settin on the porch the livelong day.
But when it came to courage,
Old Nick could stir the porridge.
They's many men would shiver when he'd say,
"A fight is jest another kind of play."

Now Miss Polly was right purty,
But as doves go she was dirty.
The one thing she demanded was her pay.
Banker Caswell he refused her.
It appeared that this amused her
For she shot him as her friends all heard her say,
"Hit's cash or you won't live no more to play."

Well the townsfolk paid no mind,
And the sheriff acted blind,
But the banker's kinfolk set up for a fray.
They come in from everwheres
On their geldings and their mares.
Old Nick jest scratched and then I heard him say,
"This fight is jest another kind of play."

They was buck-n-ball and bullet,
So nobody seen him pull it
When Nick's Walker up and started in to neigh.
In a minute they was finished
And their kin right sore diminished,
As we saw when all the gun smoke cleared away.
A fight for Nick was jest a kind of play.

Then Miss Polly she admired him.
If she could of, she'd of hired him,
But he told her as he chawed a piece of hay,
"Ain't no call to be so grateful.
Work to me is sorta hateful.
This shady porch is where I aim to stay.
Fightin now, that's jest my kind of play."

Confession to Proclivities

I have fallen in love with
the strong nuclear force constant,
which would be comforting, I suppose,
were it not for the fact that I am
equally weakened in the knees by
the weak nuclear force constant.

And I am congenial with
the velocity of light,
the average distance between galaxies
and the decay rate of protons.

If anything arouses my lust, it is
the polarity of the water molecule
in bed together with
the epoch for white dwarf binaries.

But I must confess to my most
peculiar idiosyncrasy of all:
my having become accustomed to
water's temperature of maximum density,
along with
the strength of the cosmic primordial
magnetic field,
the latter, in French, being called
le champ aimanté.

From

PSALMS OF GRATITUDE AND PRAYER

(Wipf and Stock Publishers, 2016)

Itadaki Masu

Japanese for "I have received from on high."

I have received water, flowing and pooled, salt and fresh,
   cold and hot; wind off the ocean, among the trees,
   over wheat fields; wool for warmth.
I am grateful for these, and for the many-touching octopi,
   the common beauty of oleanders, tough-limbed
   oaks, lithe ocelots, leather-skinned oranges, and
   pungent onions.
About me lie perch from farm ponds, peppers and parsnips,
   potatoes and Tellicherry peppercorns, pork and
   peaches, paprika, together with the sweet sadness
   of Pachelbel.
I have been given air to breathe, alders leafing out in spring,
   crisp apples, deep-flavored apricots, and the shield-
   like leaves of aspidistras.
Grapes and goldfinches, garlic and grass are in my treasury;
   jackrabbits and jays, ginger and juncos have come
   to me as gifts.
I am inebriated on biscuits and bass, bread and bears,
   bicycles and barracudas, on basil and brass.
Clouds and rainfall, snow and sleet, sunshine and darkness
   are my blessings, as are moonlight and firelight,
   starlight and candlelight.
I have been awarded Mozart and Bach, Verdi and Puccini,
   Homer and Shakespeare, Thomas More and Martin
   Luther, Herbert and Donne.
I have received from on high appreciative dogs and dignified
   house cats, deer and raccoons, chickens and grosbeaks,
   friendship and children, fuchsias and dahlias, soil,
   stone and steel.
May I never be ungrateful for any shelter, any mouthful of
   food or sip of water, any friendly gesture, any offer
   of help, any touch of understanding.

The Present

Small as I was, possessing like a king,
I knew my property came from my dad,
and not just some of mine, but everything.
What could I give him that he had not had?

The possibilities became a list
with statues first, then windows, then
his picture that I daily blessed and kissed.
But these were feeble objects made by men.

With Christmas drawing near, my next thought flew
to duties, proper acts of charity,
to hordes converted (to my rivals' few).
Yet which of these could I say came from me?

At last I found the box my gift would fill
and put inside the best I had, my will.

Benefits of Pain

Now comes my pain that sweeps away the world.
The cluttered workday, all the social weights,
the habit that compels on mindless day—
all gone, or hid, like minor creatures when
a monarch makes approach. The pinpoint distant
star, confronted so immense, becomes the sun,
and I am intimate with you, and dead,
for no one lives this close to all that is.

My gratitude to you who send such pain,
who melt our eyes to let us see the real,
who break our legs so we will sit and think,
who scorch our tongues so we may speak alone
of you, think none but you, see who we are
by seeing we are not the God of all.

Disaffirmation

Why is my head a stone, my heart dry wood?
Have I drunk poison and am paralyzed?
Once towering, how am I now downsized?
I creep and crouch who early marched and stood.

These are declining days of febrile light,
of wizened biceps, quadriceps of wax.
A desperate inhabitant of shacks,
I have misplaced my attitude and height.

It may be for the best. I've died before,
or almost did: on mountain roads, in slums;
when pocket-poor, while feeding on scant crumbs,
and sizing up for taste the shoes I wore.

But now at least I'm grateful for this least:
my height now grown by having been decreased.

The Comics Page

Their week is black and white, as if they slid
back every Monday to that wintry scene
before a technicolor screen had bloomed.
They're cabined also in a meager space,
obeying rules against more room or joy.

But then on Sunday all their lives are changed.
The lawns and Blondie's dress are green as hope;
the sky above Prince Valiant is pure blue.
Page after page is spread and packed with hues
like flower beds in spring, or bowls of eggs
dyed pink or mauve, yellow or chartreuse
to celebrate the new red blood of life.

To Houseguests at the Emperor's Estate

Remember always that you do not own the house.
If this fact causes you to be less careful
with its structure or its contents,
you will not be looked upon favorably.

While you may at decent intervals suggest wiser behavior
on the part of other guests, it is not your role to expel them.
The Emperor has better ways of doing so than you do.

When you are first seated at table,
your manners will be crude and offensive to other guests,
as well as to His Majesty.
This should not throw you into despair,
but it should shame you enough to learn better behavior.
Among other things,
this means never taking food from your neighbor's plate,
or drinking from her cup,
or throwing your bones in his direction.

If the servants are negligent in serving hungry guests,
you are expected to rise,
even from a place of honor,
and fetch their food yourself.
Do not be surly in this,
for the task is a higher honor than the place you rose from.

Avoid at all costs
the grave error of
accepting the Emperor's hospitality
without giving it a thankful thought.
It was given you freely,
and your freely given gratitude
will be a sign of your soul's health.

Speak little of yourself.
There are many others
better than you who remain silent.

Christmas

The earth's now near
that point of year
when Christmas is observed.
The fir tree leans,
the clan convenes
and housewives are unnerved.

There's goose and ham
and lots of Spam
so no one nice will starve.
Our Uncle Bob
has lost his job,
so mother lets him carve.

A toddler shrieks.
A baby leaks.
It's bedlam, there's no doubting.
There's so much noise
of spats and toys
it's useless even shouting.

At any rate
we celebrate
and that's the way we do it.
It's aches and pains,
and then joy wanes
so once more we renew it.

But something swell
rings like a bell
when sunlight's at its weakest.
The cosmos reels,
a church bell peals,
and strongest comes as meekest.

Acrobats

Let's all pray for acrobats,
Whose feet like goddesses' transcend
The earth as silent as a cat's
And start up toward where eagles end.

A careful foot, at angle just,
Possesses wire ten yards above
In what appears as gripping lust
But really what amounts to love.

Up high where just one slip would break
A collar bone, a leg or head,
One juggles plates for baby's sake,
Who's napping safely in her bed.

And then, eliciting more awe,
He rides the wire upon a bike
While holding on his upraised jaw
His partner, trustful as a tyke,

Who, in her turn, holds wide a bar,
A beach ball resting on each end.
Let's pray no wicked wind will mar
This lovely gift they have and lend.

For all of us are acrobats
Who juggle gratitude and tasks
While wearing shakily six hats
And try to do what heaven asks.

First Aid

What I have done to you, if I had done
to any ordinary mortal man,
would have obtained his lifelong enmity,
his plans to blast my family from life,
to leave me chained to coyotes and the ants
and curse me till he's spent his dying breath.

But you, my God, perceived in me a pale
and feeble gleam of good you lent at first.
You breathed on that weak spark until
the voices of my friends returned like bells,
and then I had just strength enough to turn
face down and abject as I begged your eye
see none of my offenses, and your ear
detect no slander from my wagging tongue.

When I had asked, I felt a cosmic nod;
you had consented to your own demand.

Tulips

Bit by bit the tulips open,
candy yellow, candy red,
shocking us with sudden brilliance,
then one day they all are dead.

Poets sing their dreary passing,
turning substance into song,
but an April thwarts their wailing,
proving all they knew was wrong.

What had seemed to us enchanting
was a moment's sharp delight.
When it fell, it went on living
deep in soil and out of sight.

Here and there the world holds letters
only thinking comprehends.
Eyes see patterned marks on paper
never wondering who sends.

Thinking sees the brilliant yellow
as the crust of hallowed bread,
and the grape as, in its essence,
wholesome and a hearty red.

Bit by bit the message opens.
Word by word we understand.
Spring by spring the tulips flourish
till they resurrect the land.

Seer

A man whose lips were blue, not from the cold
but from the words his septic spirit belched,
heard circling eagles screeching, "Read, read,"
and, opening a book, could see no print.

Instead the pages were of glass and showed
himself repellant, everything he loathed.
The screeches then transmuted to "Now speak,"
and he felt told to dance on broken legs.

He pleaded to be passed, but all that came
was an insane and molten heat that seared
his lips, his tongue, his larynx and his lungs.
Thus truly crippled, he began to sing,
which healed the cauterizing for his words.

Teach Us to Pray

after Thomas Merton

When you pray, let your tongue
taste the words it forms,
and let your mind watch the meanings forming.
This will paralyze your prayers,
but it will stop your meaningless recitations.

Next, as you pray to God,
think about his omniscience, his power,
his goodness and the problem of theodicy.
This too will stifle your prayers but,
done at other times, will cause you to pray.

Then, in times of prayer, think of your problems,
your dread of the coming day's tests,
of chores, illnesses and duties.
You may turn these distractions into petitions,
but alone they will not be satisfactory prayers.

This brings one to the asking of favors
on behalf of ourselves, our friends and the church.
This is something, but it is not enough,
for it is not focused directly upon God.
Still, even a little to One so great is much.

And then you may see through your prayer
as through a clean window, not seeing the window
but seeing God's mercy, and in that his love,
watching him adopt you as his child,
wretched child though you have been and are.

Yet still you see yourself as you pray,
and then you long to disappear, to see only God,
for your prayers no longer bring consolation
and you acknowledge for the first time that
you never loved him, but actually loved yourself.

For your love for God was a miserly love,
doled out in complacency, false modesty, conceit.

You were too self-confident, ignoring your self-delusions,
unafraid of being called a person of prayer.
Now you are terrified, and you finally regret your sins.

And now you pray, expecting nothing.
Now your pride has evaporated in the aridity.
Now any crumb of the stalest spiritual bread satisfies,
even surprises you that God should attend to you.
Now you truly pray, without knowing what you are saying.

Eucharist

*Even the dogs eat the crumbs that fall
from their master's table.*

I hear above me plates, utensils, glasses.
Their clatter punctuates the talk one uses
while eating common meals. And as time passes,
here fall the crumbs each careful diner loses.

Say I'm a dog; why give me taste for blessing
if I'm to live on what the blest are spilling?
(The stained glass sparkles; why is it so depressing?
The hymn is hearty, but the air is chilling.)

The falsely wise say feelings never count,
but in this dryness I can hear the fount
that never fails, although it seems to move.

It tells me that you never disapprove
of change, so long as it is toward your feet,
when you will lift me up and let me eat.

Side by Side

When I've moved on from here
I will remember these calm days,
the shady aconite,
the slender-legged deer,
the cherry trees
that graze on both
dark loam and sunlight.

I'll be nostalgic for the hours
spent nudging and aligning what
the Maker gave,
collaboration mingling us
so what is his is ours.
All palpable things
are like an arch through
which he seems diaphanous.

And knowing this, I almost see
his finger pointing to the needs:
weeding or a fence,
diplomacy or changing oil.
At times he will agree
they were just weeds.
At others I can sense
I've been mistaken in my toil.

But always he is there.
We make a curious pair.

The Flowering of Evil

His spirit alone was Christian. His heart and mind
remained empty.

— Anatole France on Baudelaire

Let us pray for Charles Baudelaire,
for every wastrel merits Christian care.
His "giantess," for sake of argument,
let's say was oedipal, despite intent.

And let's concede religion was a game
he dabbled in to make himself a name.
St. Wystan may be right—he may have turned
the final second of his life and learned.

So let's petition heaven he be saved
no matter how heretically he raved.
For time in heaven is not like our own;
he may not yet have reached damnation's zone.

Let's ask that in that promised world there be
a padded dwelling place for such as he.
But please be careful—rise not from your knee
before you have appended this last plea:

No matter with what volume they repent,
forbear to make such madmen president.

Kiss

The doe walks through my yard
as if it were her own.
And I suppose it is,
not being mine alone.

A useful fiction—that
we creatures can possess
in perpetuity
what's meant as one caress.

The laws of man are not
the laws of beast or God.
Who owns this cone of earth,
with stars and where he's trod?

My title to this land
will one day burn or mold
when this world's been transformed
or merely has been sold.

And yet my hope is that
what care I gave in this
brief time I have to live
will linger like a kiss.

David and Judith

When David, young and ruddy, heard the threat
Goliath posed King Saul and Israel,
he offered to remove the giant pest
as handily as he had often killed
the predators that ate his father's sheep.
One rounded stone, set whirling in a sling,
flew out and crushed the brain's soft shape.
And then the giant's sword's beheading clang.
The grown and battle-hardened warriors
were bested by a boy in God's command.

And Judith, widow, living posh indoors,
went out—instead of all her fighting men—
to outmaneuver their top general
until his wine-besotted head, adoze,
lay pillowed and convenient for the kill,
defeating his whole army with two blows.
Bethulia had agreed to drop their arms,
to offer up their town (and Israel)
should God not help them on their terms.

In just such times the lesser must do all.

Everything Is Otherwise

With all the things I've ever learned to do—
grout tile, teach literature, appreciate my wife—
I learned it just as health and age said, "Stop."

And sometimes, maybe the most crucial times,
success was just beyond my fingertips,
something I'd have grasped if I hadn't fallen dead.

But when I think of Socrates, told to commit suicide;
Lao-Tzu, his wisdom confiscated as he left China;
Da Vinci who hardly ever finished anything;

Lincoln's lead payment for preserving the nation;
and Jeshua assassinated by the Jerusalem he loved;
I begin to see that nothing succeeds if it succeeds.

The Iliad is left to scholars who seek their own fame,
and *Beowulf*'s stern syllables survive as a flashy film.
Give us failure, and let it float away like a dead king.

Let me learn to respect my son's unpromising plans,
my daughter's disastrous choice of a husband,
and my neighbor's hatred of the things I say.

Awe

We who are bereft of stately kings,
who judge each unmet person equal to
ourselves, but separate, and impotent
to tell us how we ought to live our lives;
who think ourselves courageous to deny
superiors at work a "yes" or "sir";
who grudge the admiration due the great;
we prideful insects lack the protocol
to speak to One for whom our learned books
are like the simple scratches toddlers make
when first they hold a crayon to a page.

Our skulls contain no lobes for dignity
(except our own, and none believes in that),
so majesty, the earthly kind, none can abide
(except when singing, and that's only rote).
Our souls have shrunk, these latter days, so small
there is too little room for you inside.

Expand them, Lord, till we're magnanimous.
Though Christ threw wide your doors and waved us in,
teach us to tremble as we wipe our feet.

Born Again

The man they like to emulate had said
a good reception where he lives depends
on being born again. And so they tell
of summer camp as kids, or campus groups,
or tent revivals and an altar call—
they "handed over all they had to Christ."

And I believed them, but it's puzzling when
they place such weight on what their houses cost,
or sometimes feel great pride in what they know,
or wish to keep their health, their youth, their hair.

A birth is leaving (for one's life) the womb,
the customary comforts and the warmth,
a place to lay one's head. It means to pass
one's brain case through an opening so small
the bony mind must change its shape or die.

It means a change so scary that we weep,
but weeping starts our breathing. Then we meet
the beings we had only known by voice:
she has a smell, he gives a scratchy kiss.

Look, Ananias and Sapphira died.

Containers

Forgive us, Lord, the modules of our thought,
premeasured, uniform, accepted, bought.
"Choose medium or large in taupe or black";
it's "what they're wearing," and it's in the sack.

We're woefully behind the times unless
the current topics are the ones we bless.
We draw neat lines between our foe and friend
when you yourself said wait until the end.

We're either right and brown or left and pink;
we have no sympathy with those who think
that both sides see some facts and make some sense
yet strain their insights for a strong defense.

We think we think, and seem to know we know,
until some Socrates has stooped so low
as to explain our ignorance and force
our logic back to view its bogus source.

Sometimes we try to know you as a friend,
but how can simple beings apprehend
that angry love, caress that uncreates,
who box their oranges in cornered crates,

much less who look for lions with a cage
that would not hold the tabby's minor rage.
Assuming we can stretch and still be yours,
widen our walls, we pray, enlarge our doors.

That, if we may not hold you all in all,
we may invite you in our vastest hall
and there receive your smallest finger's end.
Then we might mean it when we call you friend.

From
PERIPHERAL VISIONS

(Negative Capability Press, 2017)

Waste Baskets

Who will praise the waste cans of this world?
Mouths they are, unnoticed but for need,
standing silent like a monarch's servant,
patiently omnivorous, never
complaining audibly of needing to be emptied,
expressing their request only by
a subtle spilling of excess paper, rinds,
plastic wrappers; miming for us the message—
like a bodiless hand against our walls
writing in an indecent language—that
we have gathered dumps to our fake palaces.

"Fools," in the old tradition, the only ones
who will tell us the truth without fear of expulsion.

Scattergun

Nothing in that field was worth a word
except that it was where the old man died.
We none of us were sure of what we'd heard,
or if we said we were—well then we lied.

It wasn't like the bark his twenty gave
like he was hunting quail for New Year's Eve.
Its voice was harder, you could say "more grave,"
a season and report on which to leave.

Turned out to be the cast-aside sixteen,
the one he'd taken, cleaned, but seldom shot.
Damascus barrels, so he wasn't keen
on firing shells that might have proved too hot.

His coffin closed, we sang no cheering hymn,
but put him where he wished to be—down deep.
And then we drank until the light grew dim
and thought how soundly in the earth he'd sleep.

Soliloquy

Too many times I've urged that time should run
more lively than the sleepy clock will go.
But when the time is ripe and I reach out,
the apple proves too quick, my hand too slow.

What is impatience but a wish to fail;
what appetite but growing till we die;
what language but the stiffened mouth that says,
"I know I'm living, but I don't know why."

It is this fall, this late and autumn day
that speaks (as well as human voice can speak)
of what the Breitling watch can never tell,
and then devalues as a stopped antique.

Fish to Bipeds

A rainbow from the big-box store
is lying on our countertop,
its eye collapsed, its fins in disarray.

I'll eat of it and I will live,
which I could not now say of it,
for it was never much alive at all.

I doubt that it had even seen
a mayfly or a wooly bug.
But then it hadn't felt a piercing hook.

Maybe that's the thing that's wrong.
Life's a pleasure with some pain,
a little pain, the ordinary joys.

A society of bees,
the ripples of a living creek,
a dancer's knees, the corpse's heavy reek.

Finis

That wispy day we hardly see
is like a road trip when the haze,
as we approach, turns out to be
the mountains that betoken days
when we will weaken and our throats
will stutter like a billy goat's.

We'll walk bent over, locust-like,
and if we're able, love the child
who ran into us on his bike,
for we were once that young, that wild.
What shall we wish for on that dawn
when light goes dim and earth will yawn?

The Worship of Rapidity

Tar and concrete, asphalt, sand, and steel....
These are the gods of California. Worship them.

—Dana Gioia

The stark immensity of the steppes forced
impatient people to reduce to reins the horse.
It served us as the fastest way on earth
to plunder, then evade the pain we deserved.
Not love but rape, as the Comanches knew,
those curt successors to the Mongol brood.

A paler man, not yet in love with his wife,
would ride it till he needed to lie behind
some bulk to stop the savages' knapped stones.
Then he would look away and cut its throat,
whose loyalty he'd savored, of whose scent was fond,
who'd wrapped him in the joy of speed and wind.

But quicker than the horse, and yet less quick,
the locomotive breathed along its track,
a massive monster turned obedient—
Leviathan tamed as by a deity
with string—steel railing with some wooden steps
across the plains that sprouted soda shops,

to Disneyland, where all the life will only
look alive, and speed is time that's merely
crumpled in imagining's enslavement—
the park's time-splicing and the meld of moments.
We love the nothing we agree is there,
but if we saw the nothing, we'd be bored.

It's been a long time sapping, this withdrawal
of what lends itself to worship without
becoming something like what living people
called an idol. Pray God that Yeats saw well:
after the Beast, Reality that will elate,
not dead, unspirited, dilapidate.

Commedia Academica

Among the masked personae and their parts
are those who deify the fragile arts.
Trebissa just adores ballet and speaks
ad infinitum of the dance techniques.
Rinaldo loves the opera, and best
of all, Poulenc's "Tiresias's Breast."

Then there are those whose minds are finely honed
so, like all ancient prophets, may be stoned.
Some bow to coarser sports, buy kegs of beer,
support their teams and slap each other's rear.
Some climb the dizzy heights to thinner air
to sit in splendor as department chair.
Adina goes in boots and drives a car
a young man might afford if he were Czar
of Transylvania, or a Mongol Khan.
Pusstera is intrigued most by the Swan
of Avon, who intrudes on her pure dreams,
not frowning, but alight on lunar beams.

The worst of these is one who worships verse,
possessed by that which others deem a curse.
But lest this geniality descend
to depths where satire might offend,
we'll bring this genial poem to an end.

Emily's Corner Room

This little room, a speck of dust,
Is universe to me.
One eye looks south, the other east—
So how is one to pray?

The only living things, a clock
For pulse—and then for lungs
A Franklin that demands to break
His fast with wooden things.

And I the bottle, thin of mouth—
A ruby emptiness
Formed round to take in west and north—
And yet espoused to loss.

It must be hurricane to lift
My little world—or else
Decay bring down. I'd choose aloft
But that I lack a pulse.

For orison, these letters breathe
Totality of faith—
An indecision firm, more lithe
Than what is known as health.

A Common Man

He'd mastered how the Packard parts adhere,
just where their oily facets slipped,
and how the gasoline
combusted in a quick and clean
chain of explosions, so whichever gear
engaged, it never stripped.

He was a snob, but always in reverse.
That is to say, he loathed good style
and proved it with his shirt.
He couldn't bring himself to hurt
a soul who might turn around and reimburse
the choler of his bile.

Oh yes, he was a common sort of man,
the kind that walks down any street
and thinks he's calm and rare,
but soon he breaks her chinaware,
then orders her to make things spic and span
and, from now on, be sweet.

He fed his family and kept them housed,
it's true; and if he beat his wife,
why, she came back for more.
And so to him she merely bore
his children, cooked his meals, while he browsed
the women for a life.

Ovid in Exile

And he in Tomis, now called Rustica,
where no one lipped the Latin dear to him,
and so their ears were Scythian to wit
that budded once each era on the earth.

But barbarism has its own low pride
in pleasing spirits of abstemiousness,
perhaps because an unwashed life will lift
the status of those rules of cleanliness
till they seem irreproachable and pure.

Although he frequented the baths in Rome,
he did not, in lustrations of the flesh,
perceive catharsis of his lively lusts.
It was this heresy of theirs that brought
him to detest their sanctimony's cheer,
their base hypocrisy, Tartuffery.

Therefore he wrote to Rome his sadnesses.
Appreciations trickled in from friends,
but he had lost his audience at large,
those who survived upon the joyous life,
the pleasure in a muraled face that says
a moment's exultation or conceit,
a chiseled body in relaxed awareness.

It was the city that meant life to him,
the city where the Galilean's tribe
was even then recruiting its great host.

Whale Song

...Narcissus....that same image, we [humans] see in all
rivers and oceans.
                                        —*Moby Dick*

We who left the land behind where kin had died
have made the heaving element our halfway home
among the foreign fishes glittering with age,
unchanged for eons while we milkers form and sleeken.
Halfway home we are, in depths that had meant death
a million seasons past and puffed away, that time
we plumped across the grass savannahs, bedding down
in duskened pools and shallows, learning that to breathe
is far more precious than to eat, or than to breed.
Our limbs in atrophy, our tails a thing to smash,
we slip through water as we used to slip through air.

But then the simians arrived down from their trees,
and looked into the water's face, and saw their own.
It is the robe that Death assumes when they are called.
The White One was not one of us. He never was.
But we his mediators stand head-down to see
his artistry in luring others to corruption's bed,
had seen him spouting partridge-like away from him
who limped one-legged so as to assassinate
that shroud of death, and only murdered there himself.

The Hypocrite's Apologia

Yes, now I find I've grown too old for toys.
I've had it all and done it all. I'm tired.
These strippers bore me, and I'm not for boys.

How can it be that I had once aspired
To odalisques, each padlocked in her suite,
And billions that in minutes could be wired?

I got so far that sheepish men would bleat
To gain my smile. It ended when I tossed
My clout, and that's the day they used their feet.

But clout was not the only thing I lost.
One pleasure at a time, like peeling skin,
I shed my life into a holocaust.

And yet what's left has left me pure within,
Relieved of lusts and cleansed of every sin.

Ballade for Old Trains

They are no more, the whistles' longing wails,
Retreating like a stately, mournful queen.
Where are the smokestacks that left fading trails,
The blackened engine with its oiled sheen,
Imposing in its tons, unfazed, serene,
The ties in creosote, the polished rails?
I hear their bell, and there's a death to keen.
What lasts if such tremendous power fails?

Where will we find the heavy giant's gales
Set blowing by that massive, blunt machine?
Where are the farm boys with their silent hails,
At which the engineer will smile and lean
And wave with the importance of a dean?
Find me the cattle, timber, kegs, hay bales,
Secure and fixed, however they careen.
What can remain when such huge power fails?

And where, behind the windows and sheer veils,
Are those who dine on brook trout amandine,
On caviar, champagne and roasted quails?
Do none now bathe and dress and preen
Before they enter on the daily scene
Like those who watched the passing crags and vales,
The scree dark red, the prairies' varied green?
Endurance lies if such vast power fails.

I never would discredit or demean
Our social conscience and foreboding tales,
But cars are skits—old trains were pure Racine.
Who will remember us if such grace fails?

Valentine

Give me no villa in the south of France,
no yacht in Newport with a chandelier
and supermodels waiting at the pier,
no Hamlet role to Branaugh's Rosenkrantz.

Keep me a private man unrecognized,
my day a ritual of chores and naps,
my life a series of mistakes and gaps,
relinquishing each thing I might have prized.

But still among these losses let there be
one earthly joy, one pleasure that remains
to show those failures are a gift to me.

Let there be left one lady in my life,
a lovely one with grace, aplomb and brains,
who is my lifelong love—I mean my wife.

Inarticulate

It was the first day that I looked at you,
lascivious (as I must admit) and yet
oracular in sensing here a new
vision of a kind I thought I'd met
eons ago, and so I tried to speak.
Cables held my tongue, and hosts of words
lay peaceful in my chastened mouth and meek.
A hush suffused that holy room, while birds,
utterly undone by my still speech,
declared their singing bested in the yard.
Ever the chatterer, I could not teach
the awe within me to relax its guard.

Then decades of your cure released my tongue
enough to blurt the love I felt when young.

An Ideal Wedding

Today our friends are here to see us wed:
Our words are permanent, our time delight.
But when the cake is eaten and we've danced,
and when the wedding gown is put away,
we'll stay together, just a word apart,
in jeans and sweatshirt on a Friday night
with popcorn and a rented DVD;
or planting pansies in the early spring,
your fingers mud-caked but your eyes like stars.
When you're bent over checkbook and the bills,
I'll notice once again how soft your hair.
When you climb down the ladder, brush in hand,
you'll end up safe on earth in these two arms.
And when, in later years, your backs of hands
grow freckled as a page in rarest books,
I'll read there what is bittersweet in life:
the hard work and the jokes, the pangs of children,
the deep suffusion of parental love,
the calm good sense that comes with steadfast years,
and all the joys beginning here today.

If I'd Seen Shakespeare Sleeping

What have we here? A man or a fish?
Dead or alive?
                              —The Tempest

I would have held my breath to let him sleep,
and thought of questions for when he awoke,
and closed the window for the bleating sheep,
and wondered if he'd like a modern joke.

I'd wonder: When he wakened, would his arm
have gone to sleep? And is his sleeping breath
a thing of metrics? What would be the harm
in waking him? Does he now dream of death?

I would have paid the keeper of the inn
for his expenses—lodging, food and drink,
in case I should assume death's eyeless grin
before he might regard me with a blink

to wonder if such creatures pray and wish;
in brief, if I am corpse of man or fish.

Mountaineering by Candlelight

The path is longer than he thought.
It narrows and is laid
with sharper stones than used to be.

And now the sun beds down.
Soon it will be dark
and still the trail—
still the trail leads on,
remoter and more steep.
The cold leaks past his wool
and finds his flesh defenseless and inept.

He has a candle lantern of the sort
outfitters of the past once sold,
its flame uncertain,
light as weak as he's become,
so in this present dark, precipitous,
it shows him what there is
three feet ahead.
He could be nearly there and ignorant.

But where? He's ignorant of that as well.
He'd love to hear a human voice,
a phrase, a syllable, a word.

Old Loves

I am an older man who wears bow ties,
but lives where they elicit dulcet cries,
loves conversation when it is astute,
at times more yielding, then more absolute.

I'm all in favor of a Mozart air;
Oklahoma roses that will bear
a velvet heart and soul that's red as blood,
yet drawn from truly unimpressive mud;

a Braeburn apple, crisp, both tart and sweet,
as when both traits in debutantes should meet
avoiding both extremes, transforming each
into more meaning than a man might preach.

I love a lady with a woman's shape
who keeps it covered in a satin cape
until her first love whisks it off and sees
her graceful shoulders and her lovely knees.

A cup of coffee in the morning light,
a dram of Bristol Cream to greet the night,
four-poster bed, a book, then leap
the numbered wooly creatures till I sleep.

I am a failing man who likes bow ties
and hopes to wear one on the day he dies.

A Lovers' Spat

On summer evenings when the air is sweet
with fragrances that call to mind the past,
I wonder, will those blossom scents outlast
the night that's fallen and the fruit I eat?

How soft the music down the darkened street,
but still your lowered voice is unsurpassed
for gentle flavor in this rich repast
of essences commingled in the heat.

The music stops. Your voice has faltered, dies,
exhausted of its driving force: your lies.
One kiss to smell the rose before it's picked
and then your neck, so soft, so wide your eyes
as if it came completely by surprise
that one should know himself a cuckold, tricked.

The Edge of Light

A clearing in old growth,
a campfire at its hub,
our tents pitched all around
along the edge of light.
We lay in sleeping bags,
some telling tales
to push the dawning near
the threat of darkened woods.

The stories went around
until we mostly were
agreed that some had shed
new light upon the fire—
redundancy at best.
Some lay along the edge,
while others went too far
into the baffling dark
for us to understand,
and so brought in more dark.

We've moved our tents away
at almost every dusk
to know more of what used
to be the trackless dark.
But some still love the dark
because it seems to them
that it will make them free.
We've had no word from them,
only their gargled pleas.

The Thing with Feathers

Hope is the thing with feathers
That perches in the soul.

—*Emily Dickinson*

I.

When Homer sang his epics into form,
The bird sang weakly as a darkling thrush.
Ungrateful Agamemnon, spoiled Achilles,
"Tricks" Odysseus, Ajax "the ox"—
To these the victory. But dark destruction
Sat like thorns upon old Priam's head,
No matter that this regnant lord had bowed
And kissed the lawless hand that killed his sons,
And begged the body of by far his best,
Courageous Hector. Yes, courageous, though
He ran at last, deserted by the gods,
On whom all mortal excellence depended.
Hector, faithful to Andromache
When even Helen hints him to her bed,
Loving father of Astyanax,
Forbearing offered wine, and then resisting
Sweet advice to stay at home and live,
Returning to the field he knew was lost
To fight a man only a fop could kill.
Courageous Hector must be speared and dragged
Around the walls of civil Ilium,
The way all civil hopes (the poet says)
Are desecrated by the wild and coarse.

If age-old cities and the powerful
Who rule them kindly will be brought to dust,
Though even Zeus himself may favor them,
What hope have we in mediocrity?

II.

And then came Vergil, plucking some few seeds
Out from the loud, incinerating Troy—
Aeneas and his band—and sent them on
An odyssey until they found their Troy
In quickening reversal of its death:
As Ilium had fallen, Rome would rise.
This spoke of hope, if only that their past
Had been so noble and transcended death.
But *civitas* was all the hope they had,
Regarding Rome as typical of none
In endless reign and its eternal life.
And now it's just another capital
Where tourists can complain of being pinched.
What hope in that? Have Roman seeds developed
In another place? They have, of course,
In every place the rose is native to.
The Sower, with his feet in Palestine,
Sowed faith on Rome; and these then took advantage
Of the Roman roads and Pax Romana,
Disseminating faith around the world.

III.

In Florence, faith produced a tale to curl
Both hair and toes, in horror and in joy.
Beginning with a longing to transcend
Our petty rivalries and gnawing feuds,
The pilgrim walks beneath a portal's sign:
"Abandon every hope to enter here."
And yet he enters, yet retains some hope,
For still he casts a shadow, still can breathe;
And where there's life, one's faith can sprout, and faith
Provides the basis for a lasting hope.
Down through the earth the worm's infected way
That passes through the apple's wounded core
He passes and, at center, pivots so
In going down, he finds he's climbing up,
And up, and upward till at last he's in
The highest realm of all, the home of love,
his destiny no matter what should pass.

IV.

And what could pass? Why, everything the world
Surrounds us with and teaches us to love:
The thrill of something new, our fits of peace,
The calls of children in the growing dusk,
A spouse who can both listen and console,
A dandelion, just the smell of rain.
All these the world instructs us how to grasp,
And when we do, they melt and trickle down
Between our fingers to the porous ground.
We see this world as all because our "up"
Is really down. Our loves are pointed wrong.

And yet these smaller loves can teach us how
Some things deserve affection, teach us how
To hold them in esteem, or even awe.
And when the lesson's learned, or we
Mistake the lesson for the goal itself,
Then heroes die, and precious plans dissolve.
Our lives are shaken. If we give up hope,
We've gone no farther than the ancient Greeks
Who saw their afterlife as comatose.
The news is that there's firmer ground elsewhere
On which a city stands more real than ours,
Exactly as our host at dinner is
More real than what his table holds for us.
We may touch both, but only one responds,
And only one arranged for all the rest,
The chairs we sit on and the wine we drink.

To eyes, the future seems as random as
the oddities of nature. Wisdom, though,
Sees roughhewn patterns that apply to us.
We call it chaos, but it has a form.
And just the fact that we've been shown the shape
Is cause enough to trust the One who said
He wrote the world so that all will be well,
And everything completed will be well.

V.

Our Emily had heard it in the land
Of chill and gale, where it was sweetest to
Her nimble ear. And yet it never asked
That she repay the slightest crumb for it.
How like our Sower of the seeds of faith.
Hope perches in our souls and sings its tune,
A wordless tune, the language of the One,
Ineffable, yet clarity itself.

The Dumb Man Healed

The flames that lick along the log are like
my rootless tongue that wobbled in my mouth
that late October day when, dead to discourse,
chilled by neighbors' eyes, I stood and held
my hands out to the oil barrel's fire.
The street was dark. A wino now and then
would creep from somewhere secret like a rat
and join me in my mockery of prayer.

Please understand, we were no band of friends,
but—more like animals in drought that lose
their sense of species at the waterhole
and, predator and prey, drink side by side
the liquid possibility of life—
we held ourselves for blessing by the flames.
A mongrel sauntered by, researched each paper
bag and trashcan as a cop does doors.
That's when I saw them then a block away,
too many to fight off and yet too dressed
for any gang I'd seen. I saw them talk
among themselves while looking down at us;
it was a baker's dozen, decent in
their livery of righteous purity.
Their preacher, tall, white-haired and self-anointed,
began deploying toadies to us beasts
encircling the fire. It came to me
at once who'd started it and left the scraps
in view to keep the barrel hot all night
so we'd be many when they checked the trap.

At last he looked at me and asked me something.
How should I know what he asked? Without
a way to answer, listening just made
my tongue hurt all the more in barrenness.
He raised his hand and held it to his throat,
a sign, I thought, that surely I'd be hanged.
He came to me, his mouth a thing alive.
I told myself I'd never flinch in fear.

I breathed his soap and nearly vomited.
He raised his hand to me. I knocked it off.
He spoke like Patton, like artillery,
like tumbling skies, and so I quieted
and let him put his hand beneath
my useless chin. And that was when it happened.

Yet why should I exert myself to cough
the cornered words and tell you how it felt
to come to syllables? You breathe them as
a tree says leaves in ease along a branch.
Mine rose to voice, but rose—I can't say how—
like peach pits caught, clogged in catarrh.

It must have been the morning sun that warmed
my throat one final, crucial time, or else
relief that his so puny hand should grasp
my torsioned throat with nothing dangerous.

At all events I speak, as you can see,
though words to me are boulders I erupt;
all of them are secrets I must spit.
You sit in no more comfort than your own
and wonder if I'm grateful for my mouth,
for all that speech has given me in wealth.
What sign of gratitude would you expect?
I've made my way. This house I earned through work.
One year and everything has changed for me:
a fireplace for my fire, a chair to sit in,
coffee and some toast. Of course I'm not
ungrateful that I live in greater ease.
It's just that I'm not fool enough to run
and catch some prudish, holier-than-thou
evangelist and give him just exactly
what he wants. It's not so easy when
a man has earned society's respect.
Besides, a fellow's got to have some pride.

If Every Day Were Holiday

If I were to make the world in a jar,
I'd carefully coddle each gamete and fish,
And give tender feelings to mogul and czar,
And grant every person her whim and his wish.

The earth would be slathered in peace at all times,
With babies agiggle, with kisses and hugs,
And no poetaster would lack for good rhymes,
And every place clean, even under the rugs.

No murders, no rapes, no random mutations,
No microcephalics, no bipolar dumps,
Just carloads of kindness and endless elations.
Forget about armies; forget about grumps.

Ah, dream the bright dream, for it's certainly better
Than hardly surviving on seeds and on grass,
With leaves for a raincoat and moss for a sweater,
The life of a zebra, a horse, or an ass.

And whom would we pity? Whom would we aid?
Who could do more than pretend to enjoy
The tiresome procession of fancies we made;
Unceasing soap operas, with banquets of soy?

It's only the desperate hiding their gloom
Like idiot relatives, smelly, inept.
Some socialite wives have affairs with their groom,
And some hide the Nazis with whom they have slept.

Elephant at Our Elbow

You're in a jungle hunting elephants.
Nearby, a tree trunk seems a rarity.
And then it budges and you realize
that you are standing just a foot away
from what you searched for with binoculars.

It was that way for eons with the earth.
We gazed and wondered at the Evening Star
but had no notion that its sibling lay
beneath our feet in still proximity.
What else is much too large for us to see?

Flies

When I was young and bored, I swatted flies
and did it in the open air where more
of them came diving down at me to die
and decorate our backyard with their gore.

The more I smashed, the more I hated them
for being so prolific, for their buzz,
and for their iridescent, onyx heads.
And then an odd one changed from what it was

to something with a grain or two of thought.
I had swatted, missed and backed away.
It hunkered in a crack and there sat tight
while I stood waiting for another try.

I recognized the move. It came from fear.
But how does something with a brain of sand
detect the killing swatter when it's near?
He'd surely morphed into another kind.

This threw me off my aim. My mind went "tilt."
I think that's when I wished to be a fly.
I felt my feet and toes begin to melt
onto the floor, my geodesic eyes

revealed to me a fractured world of tiles,
my arms became translucent isinglass,
and presently the cosmos buzzed; they called
that I was "neither fly nor edifice,

but some new hybrid, something born awry,
an alien, a monster, cannibal
who's come from somewhere inconceivably high
to catch us one-by-one and eat us all."

I said I was not, and all buzzing stopped.
But soon it started in again, a sound,
a litany, a buzz that held me rapt.
It told me I would never feel a wound.

They worshiped me as monarch of the flies,
for their weak tongues made my immense commands.
I spoke like them and did so with my size,
so I was god of all their fetid lands.

But this drew youthful strength away, and I,
corrupted and dismayed, declined in state,
became their proper weight, a common fly,
the kind a boy would swat, then wait

for me to leave my safety crack so he
could slam upon my royal shape the mass
of feeble plastic and thereby to see
my flesh's disarray, his triumph crass.

From
THE INVISIBLE GOD

(Wipf and Stock Publishers, 2017)

The Blind Ones

If the bard in the Odyssey is a clue,
Homer himself was blind
but saw so clearly the Achaean ships,
the spears apparently slow in gutting a man,
the effete Trojans at their tower,
that we see them through his absent eyes.

Tiresias too, perhaps more than a fiction,
saw more than the sighted,
the running sore hidden at the heart
of Thebes, the parricide, the incest
to which others were blind until
the blindest of them all tore out his eyes
so they would see no more his offenses,
and then finally saw most truly of all.

Paul certainly, Milton perhaps.

And so we close our eyes to kiss,
and when we savor some delicious food,
and when we sleep to dream,
and when we speak to you in darkness,
hands shielding our eyes, blinded for minutes,
hoping to catch a glimpse of you.

The Camel and the Needle's Eye

The rich young man speaks

I have more sheep and goats, more houses, slaves
than Job before disaster laid him low.
My wife is out of Solomon and bears
a stair-step line of children to my fame.
But here and there I see a boil upon
the smooth skin of my life, a sign that all
may one day, in a sudden wind, collapse
and leave me naked, unprotected, shamed.

I woke some nights ago and felt the hands
of doubt, of indecision, of my youth
that gripped my neck and told me I am small.
When dawn returned (how long the night can be)
I checked my wealth and saw fragility.
So when I heard a teacher was nearby
I went to him and caught him on the point
of leaving us. I wanted some assurance
that my acts, which held to Moses' law,
were adequate to buy eternal life.

He seemed at first to ratify my goal
by listing those commands I had obeyed.
But when I said I'd kept them all my life,
he saw the wall of safety I had built
around my life: my wealth, my comfort, shield
against humiliation and decay,
and laid his hand of discourse on those bricks.
"Allow me here to tear it all away,"
he said, "and follow me to deathlessness."

At once I saw myself as stripped and shown
for children's entertainment and for fools.
I saw myself again a shameful child,
embarrassed, disrespected and debased.
These crumbs of good, I thought, had kept me warm
thus far. Why lose this good to grasp at one

that was a promise only, one man's word?
So I declined and went back to my keep
and sat among my rotting palisades.

I later heard the Romans nailed him dead,
but he revived. If that proves true, I'm lost.

Quest of the Magi

Nothing is true below the moon;
    Only the stars are wise.
That's why we blink at things of earth,
    Searching the steadfast skies.

Once we'd observed the rising star,
    Each from his proper land,
Three of us took a mount and food,
    Met as if all were planned.

On went the star, and we went on
    Following where it led.
Give no belief to those who say
    Truth will elude the head.

We had no sense where God's Son lay;
    All we pursued was truth.
When we were there we found our goal
    Lodged in a kind of booth.

Down we dismounted, knelt and gave
    Frankincense, gold and myrrh.
Herod demanded we report,
    But we did not concur.

We then returned to our homelands,
    Better for having gone.
All of us changed by truth we'd found:
    Light of the rising dawn.

Assurances

It's autumn (as the British say) when apples fall
blood-red against the whitened orchard floor,
each one an ineffective sun, too red, too small
for doing more than mime that middling star's one chore.

Enough of that. Those trees will blossom in the spring
and bear their succulence again, but we will not,
except in sons and daughters and their own offspring,
while we take to the soil to rest and then to rot.

Is there another life our souls will wake to find?
We have assurances there is, but then there are
assurances that nothingness awaits our mind,
as black and meaningless as space or fireplace char.

Where lies the fact? Is it where someone died and rose?
If people then were weak as we would be today,
they would not bet their lives on what they just suppose.
On that I'll base belief, and not on what some say.

Hand

A box of matches is a homely thing,
a drawer that's movable in which there lies
a handy squad of soldiers sleeping cold.
But fumble one to hand and scratch its head,
and it will leap to life, an ardent plasma
avid to destroy a wooden world
or light a candle's wick or else a stove.

It is no better and no worse than men
who love to build and also to destroy.
What is this cosmos but a field of gleams
that light a little while and then go cold?
What lives is temporal and loves to die.
And yet a trillion stars replace the dead.
Where is the hand that scratches their cold head?

Lepers

Because our skins are pocked,
because this renders us unclean,
because we do not wish to stain the pure,
we ring this warning bell and call, "Defiled."

We have no fellowship except
with those whose sickness shows like ours,
or did not till there came to us
the only man not leprous in the world.

He was immune to this.
It was his purity
that was contagious:
touched by him, we caught his good.

Those who stayed away
had leprosy like us
but hid it under silken ways.
And still they shun. They sicken yet.

Consummations

The mind constructs a castle
Where only huts endure
And thinks the walking cleanly
That never knew a floor.

A mountain seems a spirit
Until it's underfoot—
Then any lowland forest
Pontificates on light.

Not so the final banquet—
More like the married pair
Who know the courting frenzy
More than they did before.

To Seek Is to Have Found

He would not have inspired us to seek Him
unless we had already found Him.

—Thomas Merton

We seek I AM as bees seek scented blooms.
But bees are seeking nectar for their hive
and have already nectar nonetheless.
It's lack of recognition in closed rooms
that makes us search the fields, to scan and strive,
then find a church that promises to bless.

And when we feel that comforting surcease,
what shall we do but bow and kiss its lace?
For seeing him would strike us blind as Paul.
Let's hope that's when a nephew or a niece
will help us toward that real and living Face.
Then we will know we've always felt its call.

He's with us on our journey to meet him,
but until then our eyes are weak and dim.

Cheater's Prayer

Lord, preserve the superficial.
It's so comfy and so sweet.
Ask for nothing sacrificial,
Though we'd like our lives complete.

We prefer our coffee pallid
And our loves a trifle cool.
Our beliefs might be invalid,
But they save us from misrule.

Give us days when our attention
Never is attracted by
Anything that merits mention,
Lest our self-esteem should die.

Should the real become too forceful,
We might grimace or perspire.
Give no cause to be remorseful.
Give us hymns. Give us a choir.

Let our well-worn formulary,
All its meanings rubbed away,
Exorcise the tough and scary.
Let our dim lamps bring us day.

If this world is but illusion
And a solider exists,
Saying so would breed confusion
And amuse the atheists.

Let our lives go on unruffled,
Smoothed by miracles, until
Noise and music both are muffled
By our unresisted will.

Should a coward's courage falter,
him you pity and excuse.
Though we're braver, that should alter
Not a bit the rules you use.

We're all equal, say the sages,
So you must treat us the same.
Otherwise the Lord of Ages
Plays unfairly his own game.

Give us sunsets. Give us Bambis.
Never mind the mud and screams.
Don't think us your namby-pambies;
Just remove our horrid dreams.

From the Whirlwind

If you would speak to me as mortals utter words,
Resolve my puzzlements and clarify my world,
Tell me which party I should honor, which to shun,
Instruct me when to bellow, when to close my mouth,
Perhaps then I could walk through all my days in peace,
And everywhere I went I'd shed your healing light,
And you beside me whispering, "Do this, say that."

But when you speak, it's I who must reply to you,
And everything you ask reveals my ignorance,
And few things you award are what I had in mind.
It seems impossible to speak to One so vast,
But much more so when all my folly's understood
And you lean down to pour surprises in my ear.

No Breaking Branch

Let not this deluge of your careful gifts
contract my eye so tightly from your face.
What worse ingratitude than one who loves
the gift more than the giver's fond embrace?

It's true that, lacking these, we'd slowly die,
but lacking your affection, death would come
like sudden waves that wash away our world
and turn orations stutteringly dumb.

Give me enough for ease in my last days
as you gave me survival formerly,
but tempt me not with surfeiting, my God.
A branch too fruitful may destroy the tree.

The Invisible God

Put out the sun and douse those other stars.
That cold, disorienting black could not
come near my desolation when you turn
your face and pass unspeaking on from me.
No breath but vacuums up the smell of death.
A thought will grimace, pale and disappear.

Give me, great Maker of existence, hope,
the will to stir myself to work—some gust
of pleasure for the world, that I may know
which colored crayons sketch out my request
to lip your name and then to strew your path
with tokens of esteem. Then when you turn
and leave me once again, I may recall
the clove scent of carnations when you smiled.

Heretics

How many soldiers you have had, my God,
who went to battle for what they perceived
to be the facts concerning who you are.
Some were defeated, relegated now
to handbooks on the history of faith,
while others wrote compellingly, and so
are lionized as heroes of your church.

Subdued by violence or politics, they
felt that they defended you. Uplift them and
subject them not to Hades' gibbering.
Correct them if they erred; if they were right,
give them a robe and ring if it's your will,
and taste their praises in a hidden church.

Prayer on Going to Bed

Bolt our doors of apprehension, Spirit,
As we relinquish reason and recline.

Be you within, that toothed and leering sprites
May fear and pass unharmed our sleeping souls.

We're forced to sleep, and sleep to witness dreams,
But let them harmless come, though meaningless.

Grant also, Breath of God, that, with our strength,
Our wills may be refreshed to live in peace.

Tomorrow come, allot the day some task
That wakes a smile upon the Father's lips.

Headwaiter at Cana

When first I sipped from what the groom had brought,
it came to me how poor he was, and that,
translated, said my fee was more than he
could bear, so I resigned myself to just
a pittance of my customary fee.

As one last jug of wine was almost dry,
the servants brought out several more to me.
And this new batch, compared with what we'd had,
was as a royal gem to common stone.

The guests were tipsy from the sour wine.
How could they taste, and how appreciate,
this subtle but delicious quaff? I voiced
my puzzlement at his reversing of
tradition's hospitality, and yet
his answer never reached my careful ear.

When all of them had stumbled home in something
toward an ecstasy, a servant told
how one impressive guest had turned the full
capacity of water to that most
delicious wine. So I suppose that untaught
explanation must at last suffice.
But I suspect the host was not as poor
as I'd supposed. Yet still the serving order
is a puzzlement. Oh well, it's not
as though such oddities do not occur.

Agape Champion

What insolence, to ask if I can love.
Of all those you might ask, you come to me?
I, who teach the others by the way
I live, my arms spread wide for that embrace
the sage apostle said to give our friends?
My face will ache when I relax at home,
the thorn that follows days of rosy smiles.

And everyone I love I then forgive,
and then forgive again when they return
my love with snide remarks and filth in words.
Four hundred ninety times the Lord commands
we wipe remembering's painful slate of those
offending us. My worst offender gave
two hundred forty-two. I still forgive.

I would not like to think of his demise,
the boiling pitch up to his nether parts,
huge hornets stinging lips and eyes, the roar
of hard-rock music always in his ears.
No, I should like to see him smiling when
at last he sees the love that passed him by.
It's that I pray for, that I beg to see.

Assuming you're aware my Emma's gone,
you must have heard how loud I wept.
She cooked, she cleaned. It's true she criticized,
but that's all right. I grinned and shrugged it off.
I hardly think of it these days at all.
I wept for love, and just before she went,
I said to smile and took her photograph.

I made her happy, that much I can prove.
Her smile reflected love I always gave.

The Incarnate One Himself

You want to walk the dusty roads with Jesus,
talk with him about your rheumatism,
ask him why your newborn daughter died,
make suggestions as to things he said
that trouble you, that just sound wrong.

And then you watch him stand and puzzle out
an answer to the woman and her crumbs.
You sniff the odor of a man on a hot day.
You notice that, on a boat, he sits on a cushion.
You see lice in his hair, uncut toenails,
dirty hands at a meal, sharp words to lawyers.

Do you still wish to be near, to know him?
Or would you rather meet him on a clean page,
in an archaic translation, with footnotes?

Making Predators

The world is rich with hamsters, rats and mice,
the vegetarians whom Dr. Spock
envisions as the future racial stock:
industrious, bucolic, little, nice.

We see them nibbling barley, nuts and rice.
But look where, coiled and mottled as a rock,
one hopes to slip his body like a sock
down over head and hips—a meal concise.

And you, my friend—with Beemer, houses, cash,
no more ideal than you are small and cute—
create the dragon on your gleaming stash.

This is no wish for harm. I pray the brute
will starve and you get nothing worse than rash.
But history's a slut, and so is loot.

Church

The little country church is painted white,
White as the snow around it this cold day,
And so its heavy iron bell must play
A shadowed sound across the blinding light.

But in the church a woodstove blushes hot,
As do the saved, embarrassed by their past,
Contrasting with this good beyond their caste,
As if they'd won a mansion or a yacht.

So there the upright Baldwin belts a hymn
As colorful as awe and skills allow,
Each woman like a blossom-laden bough,
The trunk-like husbands dressed in gray, and trim.
The world is cold, demands a face that's grim,
But still the church is warm, at least for now.

Churchgoing

Tomorrow is a Sunday morning
and once again the switched-on smiles,
assurances that we are not gnashing
our teeth on the frailties of others.
Again the sense that the Father
is pleased by our being here at all,
but would prefer we sang and prayed
with him in mind.

Again we sit expecting entertainment,
a play on Word, something understood,
a note of mystery, Eleusinian perhaps,
displaying us as having died and now
risen with a jolt of liveliness,
making us feel we could fight off any foe,
huge python or atheist,
and live like a pagan hero to boast of it.

A little better to go home afterward,
consider the blessing of our spouse
and offer our gratitude to the Lord.

A Gem Reset

Someone found a diamond,
a huge and lustrous thing.
It formulated light,
made it visible music.

The salesmen set it
in ordinary gold
with lesser gems.

But the gold wore thin,
and the everyday jewels
fell in the dust.

Still they kept the diamond,
reset it in silver,
a plain foil
for a precious stone.

When the silver tarnishes,
others will set it in bronze,
until one day its irons crack
and it will be known as Hope.

Sunday Morning

The oak pews are empty,
too early for people to arrive.
But the worn places and scratches are honorable.
They are ready to receive more of
the timid, watchful girls and their restless brothers,
the casual adults in their jeans,
the older men in coats and ties,
and the octogenarian ladies in sweaters.

The flowers on the altar have been given
in memory of someone most have never met.
A professional florist would not be satisfied,
but everyone who comes will think them fine.

Singly and in pairs the members amble in,
never quite filling the place.
Then the piano reminds us of the rustic tune,
and the voices, unsure, trembling,
rise up like a flock of birds,
always intending to reach the sky
but never realizing how far away it really is,
never realizing, either, that the gesture is enough.

The Wedding Feast at Cana

Although it covers one entire wall,
The guests and hangers-on spill out the sides,
For Veronese could not make it hold
The great, unruly number who, with Christ
In hearing, still would prattle of the food,
The chance of rain, migrating birds, or tell
The story of a bunion's agony.

They are, of course, a little drunk by now,
The host just tasting what a wine should be.
But no one's had a drink when we allow
Whole days to be consumed with choosing clothes,
Or training grass to do a carpet's job,
While somewhere in the house there sits the Man
Who stares unheeded deep within our eyes.

Gifts of the Spirit

Some run the buzzing vacuum, some a cloth
To polish oaken pews until they gleam;
One hand waters rhododendron trees,
Another digs to plant azaleas,
While in the office someone types and files
And takes the interrupting call with ease,
And someone else replaces bulbs that light
The place where we give ringing thanks for light.
Around a table sit the councilors
Adjudicating where finances go,
While several household kitchens make the air
Delicious with the smells of stews and loaves
For hungry worshippers on Wednesday nights.
Some wash and press the snowy altar cloth,
While others see that there is wine and bread.
Some carry logs to pile and set aflame,
Making the fireplace bright, the faces warm,
While others fill the urn for coffee cups.

From different parts of town the greeters come
And stand outside the doors to welcome in
Familiar faces and some searching ones.
From different parts the punctual ushers come
To take the offerings and tally them.
Some make the organ speak or call in zeal,
Or the piano strike its tensioned cords,
Releasing pent-up music on the air.
Then those who sing like morning birds are heard,
And those of us who sound like barnyard hens
Admix our tinny voices to the song,
Which heaven alchemizes to bright gold.

Then someone leaves her pew and reads to all
Some passages from that immortal Book.
And then the Pastor's voice speaks to his sheep,
Who recognize its tones and stand alert;
The news is good—they strain to hear each word.

And then the sermon, gloss upon the text,
A guided meditation on the Word,
A loving blend of thought and urgency.

Soon worshippers go altarward to eat
And drink as Christ's apostles did
That fatal night the world devoured his life,
The pastor's hand distributing the bread,
Some others sips of lifeblood from the grape.
In other rooms the children sit and hear
Of Samson's hair and David's sling, and how
Our Lord invited children to approach.

All these add what ability does best,
The drum or tuba to the symphony,
The wiring, pipes and windows of a house.
Although the wires are live, the pipes are full,
The windows let in light, no frowning porter
Guards the door to keep us few in joy,
But ventures out to bring the wayward in,
For still the Wedding Feast has empty chairs.

Hearing God

Among the stacks of books he gave away
Was one entitled *How to Hear Your God.*
His wife had bought them, seeking ways to pray,
To love, to see his face—she of the nod,

Or when awake, the single word, the smile.
He stows her walker when they've reached their pew,
Then sits himself beside her near the aisle
Where he can hear and nothing blocks her view.

The prayers and sermon pass her mind like air,
But she hears something; her attentive face
Is clear on that: initially the scare,
And then the strain to hear the tones in bass.

The books are useless now; they've sown their seeds.
We watch and see how he'll fulfill our needs.

Close Shave: A Western

The killer lay back in the barber's chair,
His face in lather like a mad dog,
His neck exposed to the straight razor.
The barber knew of the good men killed,
The widows left with their hungry young,
Those young who were left, their throats uncut.
The others will never say what he did
While their mothers watched in the ransacked house.

So the razor hung in the air above
The throat the girls had seen at close range.
But the killer knew, and he smiled to know
That a man will live with a bleeding throat
Just long enough to draw and fire,
And he knew the barber knew it too.
So the barber shaved the killer's face,
Who paid him nothing and left with a sneer.

But few of us would die to end
The anguished deaths of homespun folk.

A Civil Reply to Screwtape

[God] has made change pleasurable to them....
But since He does not wish them to make change...
an end in itself, He has balanced the love of change
in them by a love of permanence.

—The Screwtape Letters

I love a change of pace, a change of scene,
But when I've lost my way among the new,
I find the same old thing makes me serene.

A flat stability is much too clean;
I long to rove, to taste, to live askew
And love the change of pace, the change of scene.

But then adventure soon becomes obscene;
I trade the seascape for my kitchen's view,
Because the same old thing makes me serene.

You demons bait your hook with flash and sheen,
And scheme to net and land and kill us through
Our love for change of pace, for change of scene.

But heaven's planted here a sweet routine
Of table, of our bed, and of a pew.
We know these same old things make us serene.

Our saving grace is that we live between
Those ancient trees and these that lately grew.
We love a change of pace, a change of scene,
But only in the old are we serene.

UNCOLLECTED POEMS

Jonah

I plopped me down, bedraggled, failed and pooped
with prophesying to an earless mob.
The day was hot. The fig tree shaded me.
Just drifting off when, "BIRD," he shouts and breaks
my nap and nearly eardrums all in one.
It is his nickname for myself (I'm Dove)
for being hesitant to plow the sand.
"Scoot off to Nineveh," he thunders on
(or words to that effect), "that monstrous burg,
and tickle ears with this: I know their tricks."

Oh, Nineveh, says I to me, the town
that crawls with hookers and their ruttish queen.
When halfway decent Jews told me, "Get lost,"
my first reaction should have been, "Aha,
why not the Ninevites? They worship God
[wrong one, of course]. Smooth sailing all the way."
Good luck on his new enterprise, I thought,
and hopped a tub in Joppa that was aimed
at Tarshish, just as far from Nineveh
and his great larynx as a ship can sail.

But, oh, the ocean. I had thought it flat.
It turned that day to perpendicular.
The scow was buckling, so the gobs began
to yell for different gods, their favorites:
Ahura Mazda, Baal, Poseidon.
I was below, continuing my nap
and breathing in the perfume of the bilge,
but I could tell their empty prayers had failed,
so then I heard the splashes as they dumped
their lading overboard. That failed as well,
and down the boatswain came to throw me too,
or so I thought. It happened that he said
to get to praying to my god. Yes, right,
thought I. I pay this swabbie to transport
my carcass miles away from Yahweh's voice,
and presto! he says ask for Yahweh's voice.

But things were frantic. He went off to say
they had to find the skulking guilty guy
who was aboard and causing all the fuss.
They had to draw the lots. And, true to form,
the lots said me. I got the third degree.
They recognized my scheme, so I said, "Me."
They weren't the swiftest boys to catch a thought,
so I gave it another word or two:
"You threw the rest of it. Now throw me in."
But all that got was funny looks, as if
I'd come out here because I liked to drown.

But rowing hard for shore (their next device)
proved just as futile as the rest, so then
they prayed to Yahweh to forgive them for
deep-sixing me. I sailed (this time without
a deck to touch my feet) beyond the rail
and made another splash, and sank below
their voices and below the world of bread,
below the light. I hadn't thought the dead
would own such popping eyes. They stared
at me descending like a wounded bird,
as if I had disturbed some protocol.
But (shall I say it?) I was glad to be
so taken off. It meant I was beyond
his call, his reach, his chores that never worked.

But, oh, the deeps! I'd sought oblivion.
I got instead solidity of loss.
Here was no sense, no up or down, no straight.
There seemed no bottom to abhorrences.
Their teeth surrounded me, and every mouth
that gulped me down disposed me farther from
the everyday comestibles of life
with Yahweh and the world of sense he gave.
I prayed. He heard. I cast up on the shore.

I was where I had started. Then the Voice:
"Get up, you avian recalcitrance."
Caught resting once again. And so I went.

I got to Nineveh, a stinking dump.
I found a corner, went through my routine,
the forty days of leniency, the threat.
It tumbled from my mouth. I hardly heard
the words myself, so useless did it seem,
so misdirected to a mound of muck.

I should have known: the hardest heads of all,
the lushes, lechers, whores, the murderers,
whose conscience never twinged to rob the sick
or hold the wages of an honest man,
these, *these* repented. These turned sweet at once.
I'd thought their ears were fortresses. Instead,
they dropped like ripened figs, and just as sweet
in Yahweh's mouth. It was as usual:
He's tender and compassionate. It takes
an eon for his anger to build up.
And all it takes to stop this building up
is stopping what you've done and giving in.
I told him so. I'd had enough of it.
I also said I'd had enough of life.

I went off where the morning sun shone on
the city's filth and made myself a shade,
a gimcrack shelter where I sat and watched
to see if he would raze that pile of trash.
But nothing happened to the town. It was
my hair he twitched again: a castor bean
took root and filled the holes the sun looked through.
I almost laughed. Now this was more my style.
It lasted just one day. The following,
it withered, and my anger heated up.
Was I his bird? Would I have treated birds
the way he scorched his prophet's balding skull?
I ground my teeth. I clenched my fists and growled.
And then like purling water he spoke soft:
"Upset by nothing more than this? A plant
you never planted, one that lives one day?
And why should I not grieve for Nineveh,
this city of a hundred thousand souls?"

Age and the Age

These are the days of common hearing aids,
of CPAP machines to breathe at night,
of losing weight we've never gained before.

The days of self-made vows for honesty
too strict for the wavering likes of us
and the occasional lies we've spat.

The days of attraction to an earlier day in
selected memories. They're varnished.
They ordinarily stank; we'd recoil now.

The era of our lives is neither better
nor worse than those before.
Because apples rot somewhere yearly,

yet violin prodigies rise to play our thoughts.
This mix allows for widespread survival
while nourishing the gene for hope in us.

The Mirror Pond

I won't bore you with an account of how
the pond was named, its placidity or its form.

All I will say is that we lived on its
western bank, the morning sun dazzling
our eyes until we instinctively shut our lids.

Often this ushered us into dreams of scudding
over holes in the earth too large for planes to
safely cross, no matter how calm the weather.

I remember one dream in particular in which
the downdraft pulled a cloud so low it
blanketed the opposing bank of a hole in fog,
enough to instantly inspire a forest's growth.

It seemed to be oaks, but I couldn't be sure.
Then as the fog arose to a cloud again, the trees
disappeared. I wish I could recall the rest of it.

Such dreams lulled me into a sense of security,
tranquility actually—a sense that all would be well.
When I awoke the sun was gone and the pond
was spangled with flaming diamonds.

I understood, for a moment, nearly everything.

Secret Smoker

She has a cache for her cigars,
her matches, nipper, humidor,
all nestled safely in a box
of figured oak and ancient brass.

Partaking fiercely every day,
she draws it down into her lungs
and feels the flame that lit the smoke.
Now who am I to give advice?

But something else that's hidden might
be prompting her to die next year.
I won't say what, but somewhere safe
she keeps some letters from her wife.

On Sunday mornings, she recalls
the pastor of a megachurch
explaining how she'd lose her soul.
And then she takes another puff.

Acknowledgments

Grateful acknowledgment to the editors of the following serial publications where these poems were first published.

Beyond the Pillars: "Artemis"
Blue Unicorn: "Consummations," "Inarticulate"
Bohemia: "Arthur on Lancelot"
Common Ground Review: "Mountaineering by Candlelight"
Cowboy Poetry Press: "Nasty Nick"
Image: "Teach Us to Pray"
Legends: "The Wolf People"
Literature and Belief: "Eulogy"
Midnight Circus: "The Nurse in the *Odyssey*"
Pea River Journal: "Whale Song"
Radix: "The Edge of Light"
Relief: "Itadaki Masu," "Everything Is Otherwise"
Shooters Magazine: "Scattergun"
The Lyric: "Valentine," "No Breaking Branch," "Finis"
The Penwood Review: "Eucharist"
Poetry Church Magazine: "Acrobats"
Time of Singing: "Church"
TRINACRIA: "Fish to Bipeds," "The Hypocrite's Apologia"
Zingara: "This Is Not a Marriage"

About FutureCycle Press

FutureCycle Press is dedicated to publishing lasting English-language poetry books, chapbooks, and anthologies in both print-on-demand and Kindle ebook formats. Founded in 2007 by independent editor/publishers and partners Diane Kistner and Robert S. King, the press incorporated as a nonprofit in 2012. A number of our editors are distinguished poets and writers in their own right, and we have been actively involved in the small press movement going back to the early seventies.

The FutureCycle Poetry Book Prize and honorarium is awarded annually for the best full-length volume of poetry we publish in a calendar year. Introduced in 2013, our Good Works projects are anthologies devoted to issues of universal significance, with all proceeds donated to a related worthy cause. Our Selected Poems series highlights contemporary poets with a substantial body of work to their credit; with this series we strive to resurrect work that has had limited distribution and is now out of print.

We are dedicated to giving all of the authors we publish the care their work deserves, making our catalog of titles the most diverse and distinguished it can be, and paying forward any earnings to fund more great books.

We've learned a few things about independent publishing over the years. We've also evolved a unique, resilient publishing model that allows us to focus mainly on vetting and preserving for posterity poetry collections of exceptional quality without becoming overwhelmed with bookkeeping and mailing, fundraising activities, or too-taxing editorial and production "bubbles." To learn more about what we are doing, please come see us at www.futurecycle.org.

The FutureCycle Poetry Book Prize

All full-length volumes of poetry published by FutureCycle Press each calendar year are considered for the annual FutureCycle Poetry Book Prize. This allows us to evaluate each submission on its own merits, outside of the context of a contest. Too, the judges see the finished book, which will have benefitted from the beautiful book design and strong editorial gloss we have become famous for.

The book ranked the best in judging is announced as the prize-winner in the subsequent year. There is no fixed monetary award; instead, the winning poet receives an honorarium of 20% of the total net royalties from all poetry books and chapbooks the press sold online in the year the winning book was published. The winner is also accorded the honor of being on the panel of judges for the next year's competition; all judges receive copies of all contending books to keep for their personal libraries.

www.ingramcontent.com/pod-product-compliance
Lightning Source LLC
Chambersburg PA
CBHW072142090426
42739CB00013B/3262